T0017233

Re/Inventing Journalism to Strengthen Democracy

Insights from Innovators

Edited by Paloma Dallas and Paula Ellis

The Charles F. Kettering Foundation, headquartered in Dayton, Ohio, is a nonpartisan, nonprofit, operating foundation rooted in the American tradition of inventive research. Founded in 1927 "to sponsor and carry out scientific research for the benefit of humanity," the foundation is inspired by the innovativeness and ingenuity of its founder, the American inventor Charles F. Kettering. For the past four decades, the foundation's research and programs have focused on the needs of democracy worldwide.

Reinventing Journalism to Strengthen Democracy is published by the Kettering Foundation. The interpretations and conclusions contained in the book represent the views of the authors. They do not necessarily reflect the views of the Charles F. Kettering Foundation, its directors, or its officers.

Copyright © 2023 by the Kettering Foundation

ALL RIGHTS RESERVED

For information about permission to reproduce selections from this book, contact info@kettering.org.

This book is printed on acid-free paper. First edition, 2023
Manufactured in the United States of America

ISBN (print) 978-1-945577-67-3
ISBN (ePDF) 978-1-945577-68-0
ISBN (ePUB) 978-1-945577-69-7
Library of Congress Control Number: 2022920873

Contents

Foreword

by Sharon L. Davies

The state of democracy today is of urgent concern to the Kettering Foundation and our allies and partners. Almost nightly, we hear distressing reports of social divisiveness, which undermines democracy, and we see signs that some people prefer to foment division and instill fear of others instead of encouraging the cross-cultural understanding and consensus-building essential to a democracy. We see an erosion in the rule of law, waning public confidence in democratic institutions, and the loss of democratic norms—the "soft guardrails of democracy." And we have seen attacks on our free and independent press in its watchdog role. In response to these threats, we've seen institutions like the free press amplify efforts to evolve to meet this crisis.

In November 2022, Pulitzer Prize-winning journalist Nikole Hannah-Jones launched the Center for Journalism & Democracy at Howard University with the critical mission of "strengthening historically-informed, pro-democracy journalism." The center aims to reshape the field of investigative journalism by infusing it with a diversity of perspectives and lived experiences that have long been underrepresented in journalism and by departing from approaches that rely heavily on unrealistic notions of objectivity and neutrality. At the center's inaugural Democracy Summit, Hannah-Jones gathered an audience of journalism students, mostly from historically Black colleges and universities, journalists from an inclusive cross-section of media outlets and newsrooms, and panelists whom she described as representing "the diversity of America." Framing the summit's discussions, Hannah-Jones charged the audience: "The American people depend on us to be a watchdog over our democracy and to expose the continuing efforts to subvert it. And so the times demand that we liberate ourselves from the old conventions about journalism."

The contributions that Paloma Dallas and Paula Ellis have assembled in this important collection are the products of the Kettering Foundation and our partners grappling with the old conventions of journalism and developing innovative interventions in service to strengthening our democracy. The contributors offer insights fundamental to the work of reinventing journalism. They ask questions about democratizing access to the tools of storytelling; they dissect the relationship between power, truth, and journalistic neutrality; and they explore journalism through the lens of connection and belonging.

At the Kettering Foundation, a pro-democracy, operating research foundation, we believe deeply in the potential of the free press to inform, empower, and unify by adding texture, shape, and clarity to the challenges facing democracy around the world. I'm deeply grateful to Paloma and Paula for their leadership on this collection of insights and to each of the contributors for their commitment to our democracy.

Sharon L. Davies
President and CEO
Kettering Foundation

Introduction
by Paloma Dallas and Paula Ellis

Recent years have laid bare how fraught and fragile democracy's promise is: the idea that a people, with all their differences, can together chart a shared future. That they can do so with empathy and collective wisdom. That they can trust their institutions to be vehicles for self-governance. And, finally, that they can see one another as equals, recognizing their own agency while tempering their actions with the recognition that others have agency, too, ever mindful that we are in this together, our destinies intertwined.

To expect all this of any one of us, let alone all of us, is a big ask.

But it is the fundamental promise of a democracy. It is the promise of one person, one vote. It is the exhilarating ambition of "We the People," even if it has never been fully realized.

In a democracy, each generation is asked to revisit the decisions of those who came before them, remedy errors, tackle problems long left unresolved, and confront unforeseen challenges.

To help members of the public do this work of self-governance responsibly, and knowledgeably, is what journalists are called to do. It is why the role of a free, independent press was deemed so essential to democracy that it was enshrined in the First Amendment to the US Constitution. The founders knew that the fledgling

American republic's experiment in democratic government needed the free circulation of information and ideas to survive. As Thomas Jefferson wrote, "Were it left to me to decide whether we should have a government without newspapers, or newspapers without a government, I should not hesitate a moment to prefer the latter."[1]

In this collection of essays, the authors, all journalists, reflect openly and honestly on their attempts to find ways that journalism can better serve democracy. Their reflections offer insights into how journalism, with shifts in its professional mind-set and practices, might help repair our civic fabric and strengthen democracy, a task that has seldom felt more urgent.

As this book was coming together, worries about the future of democracy in the United States moved from academic sanctuaries to city streets, from neighborhood bars to corner bodegas and the bleachers of suburban soccer fields. Each day's news brought another in a seemingly endless wave of reports about racial injustice, police brutality, political malfeasance, disregard for the rule of law, and example after example of how one democratic institution or another was failing the people. While some leaders preached their belief in the search for common ground, their hopeful messages seemed muted against the timbre and intensity of the discord.

Americans do agree on one thing: a 2022 public opinion poll found that 69 percent of both Democrats and Republicans think "the nation's democracy is in danger of collapse."[2] No doubt their reasoning differs, but agreement on this stark assessment is worrisome.

People's confidence in all kinds of institutions, including in the three branches of the federal government, has diminished. While this trend has been a long time in the making, it has hit new lows with only

25 percent reporting trust in the Supreme Court, 23 percent in the presidency, and a mere 7 percent in Congress.[3] Trust in the media to report the news fairly has similarly declined, further weakening an embattled industry beset by rapidly changing technology, an advertising-based business model that internet competitors disemboweled, and the shifting news consumption habits of people who now have many more information options.

While people have more access to information than perhaps ever before, the sheer volume and speed at which it travels makes it more difficult to discern its validity, and the fragmented media ecosystem has contributed to the fracturing of the body politic. Recognizing and solving shared problems seems more difficult than ever.

Yet solve them together we must. Our ability—or inability—to collectively participate in self-governance is the central democratic challenge that journalists address in this book. They recognize that the nitty-gritty work of democracy is rooted in the daily actions of citizens who eschew highfalutin theories in favor of practical solutions. They aren't nostalgic about a golden age of journalism or democracy; they dissect lessons of the past as they respond to the challenges of today. While these authors respect the critical role the press must play in holding elected officials and others in power accountable to the public, they are concerned that it is not enough.

In this book, the authors speak to the practical work of a democratic citizenry that undergirds our system of representative government and elections, and they reimagine how journalists might work *with* this democratic citizenry. They're not just imagining though. These authors recognize that this time of tumult and questioning creates opportunities to experiment with putting new ideas into practice.

The authors, some of the nation's leading innovators in journalism, are accomplished storytellers who understand the power of narratives to shape the way we see ourselves and understand one another. They are exploring the role journalism might play in creating a narrative of American identity that is more equitable and inclusive, reflective of a broader and ever-evolving sense of ourselves as a people. Rather than stand apart from communities to report *on* them, they want to work and report *with* people, recognizing that as journalists they, too, have a stake in thriving, equitable communities. They want to contribute to building trust, not only with the media but also between people, and they see a profound role to play in fostering a sense of belonging so that all people in this country see themselves as part of the democratic experiment.

The journalists whose essays appear in this collection participated in meetings at the Kettering Foundation, beginning in 2016. That year, trust in the media in the United States had hit a historic low, with only 32 percent reporting "a great deal" or "a fair amount" of trust in the media. The decline in trust was especially steep among Republicans, with only 14 percent reporting trust in the media, a precipitous decline from the 32 percent who had reported they trusted media just a year earlier.[4]

Rather than initially focus on building or rebuilding trust, we centered our meetings around the simple question that the Kettering Foundation asked for years: What does it take to make democracy work as it should? Then, we asked about the implications of the answer for journalism. What more, or what else, is required of journalism as an institution to strengthen our democracy and ensure it serves the interests of all people?

The journalists gathered periodically at the foundation's Dayton, Ohio, campus and on Zoom to identify the problems of democracy and of journalism that most concerned them. Many had already begun to experiment with a wide range of innovative ideas that challenged existing journalism orthodoxy. Over the course of a few years, we met regularly and learned together. The journalists reported on their efforts. Sometimes they succeeded; sometimes they fell short. Regardless of the outcome, we asked them to tell us, and each other, what they had learned. Foundation folks, drawing from decades of scholarly and practical research, added to the mix.

In this book, we step back to offer all these innovators an opportunity to deepen their own understanding and ours by writing about their learning journeys. In the essays, the authors mine their experiences for insights and inflection points, for flashes of comprehension and the slower slog of sense-making. We hope their stories suggest entry points for others—both journalists and non-journalists—to launch experiments. We think small-*d* democrats everywhere might view these journalists as allies in fashioning new narratives about our collective identity and in creating a more constructive public square.

Precisely because these innovators have mastered the craft, they are able to imagine what could be done differently and credibly invite others to join them in reinventing journalism to better serve democracy. That said, this book is not a roadmap for fixing journalism. And it doesn't purport to offer a tool kit of any sort. Instead, it offers a candid assessment of journalism's relationship to democracy. In fact, it offers 10 such assessments. As the authors in this collection take stock of their profession and how we have landed at this point of deep distrust—of each other, of the media, and of institutions of all kinds—they also offer ideas about ways forward.

The authors take on journalistic "objectivity," the overreliance of the media on experts and institutions, and the tendency toward an extractive relationship with the public. They also take on perceptions of who "belongs," how this has shaped mainstream media culture, and what that has meant for democracy.

They raise pivotal questions that shifted their own thinking.

For David Plazas, it was: "Why should I trust you?"

For Martin Reynolds: "Are you going to be sustainers, creators, deniers, facilitators, or dismantlers of systemic racism?"

For Linda Miller, they were questions she asked of others: "What does it sound like, look like, and feel like to be accurately represented in the media? How would more accurate racial narratives influence how you experience public life and decision-making?"

The volume opens with an essay by Subramaniam Vincent, who directs Journalism and Media Ethics at Santa Clara University's Markkula Center for Applied Ethics. Vincent describes how journalism has evolved together with liberal democracy, with both now facing pushback around the globe. American journalism's claim and ability to support democracy is undercut, he argues, not only by the destruction of its business model and the challenges brought on by the internet and social media but also by a journalistic culture shaped by dominant White cultural norms and a "proximity to elite power and official authority and at a relative distance from the democratic agency of the people." He builds his essay toward a series of suggestions for how journalism might "reclaim its democratic potential." They include newsrooms recognizing a hierarchy of values, understanding that some—such as dignity, equality, fairness, and justice, for example—are absolute, while neutrality must always be qualified: "Neutrality toward whom? Neutrality to what end?"

Doug Oplinger, former managing editor of the *Akron Beacon Journal*, who later led a statewide media collaborative in Ohio, takes readers on a journey that spans a half century. His evocative descriptions lead the reader from the bygone era of "fuzzy black and white televised images" to today's chaotic and often discordant media ecosystem. Throughout the twists and turns, Oplinger held fast to his enduring commitment to the communities he served and experimented with different ways of engaging them while fending off accusations of advocacy or "boosterism." He draws a contrast between such experiments and the extractive "parachute journalism" that has led many citizens to believe that the media doesn't care about them. Journalism, he writes, "should be integral, vital, living threads in the fabric of democracy, stretching and flexing so that people see us as partners, as vital to improving their lives."

Michelle Holmes, former vice president of content with Alabama Media Group, begins her essay with a lyrical encapsulation of how to recognize a healthy democracy. It depends on "whether its people use 'we/ours' or 'they/theirs' when they speak of public life," she writes, before exploring the role newspapers have historically played in creating a sense of belonging for many, even as they excluded others. Holmes details a series of efforts to help foster an inclusive sense of belonging. That, she writes, is where the future of journalism lies. The news media must be "something greater than tellers of tales, compilers of facts, or uncoverers of injustice." Rather, they must be mirrors that allow "humans to see themselves in relation to the whole, and to feel their own place inside of it."

Martin Reynolds, former editor in chief of the *Oakland Tribune* and co-executive director of the Maynard Institute, also takes up the idea of "belonging" in an essay that begins with his tears of rage while watching the video of a White Minneapolis police officer kill George Floyd by pinning the unarmed Black man to the ground with his knee. Reynolds explores the tension between his training as an "objective" reporter and his experiences as a Black man with a Black son. He writes of his efforts to bring new perspectives to the paper's community coverage, with the founding of Oakland Voices as one prescient example. And he draws on his experience as a musician to suggest how dismantling systemic racism in newsrooms might truly foster a diverse and inclusive sense of belonging that can radiate out "through the shifting of the journalistic gaze, away from Whiteness, to the kaleidoscope of gazes that reflect our society and our world."

Jennifer Brandel, cofounder of Hearken, wants to help remake journalism so that it is fundamentally responsive to people, rather than mediated by the editorial sensibilities of the newsroom. Journalism's routines, she writes, are rooted in the machine age, when information was scarce and "newsrooms competed with one another to be the go-to source for truth." In the digital age, we're oversaturated with information. In response, Brandel founded Hearken, a public-powered journalism company, which is but one of the companies she has created in an effort to change the culture of journalism into one that fosters cooperation, transparency, and responsiveness to the people it serves. She imagines a system in which journalists are "incentivized to support collective sense-making, or to distribute the responsibility for care within a community, or to provide a forum for people to find common ground and other like-minded people to take civic action." Brandel describes experiments that begin to make this paradigm shift.

Ben Trefny, interim executive director of KALW Public Media serving the San Francisco Bay Area, begins with his experience anchoring live coverage of the 2016 presidential election results. After Donald Trump was declared the winner, one of Trefny's guests commented that he now felt like a stranger in his own country. Trefny responded, "Clearly a lot of people already did." "In a democracy," he writes, "the people—all the people—are supposed to govern themselves. So, it fails when entire communities are misrepresented or excluded by those who wield power and influence. Journalism contributes to that failure." Trefny chronicles his radio station's efforts to better connect with the diversity and complexity of the communities it serves, sharing the missteps and opportunities that emerged along the way. His takeaways include the power of partnering with other journalism organizations, the importance of connecting with organizations in the community, and the conviction that journalism is best practiced with the people.

Eve Pearlman writes about what led her to cofound Spaceship Media and its dialogue journalism approach. It was created, she writes, in response to the coarsening and dehumanizing of so much political rhetoric. "Our journalistic institutions were doing what we had always done, even as the landscape was changing," she writes. What could journalists do to support and create an informed public whose members can engage with one another about the issues that matter in a democracy? How could she combine her moderating and mediating skills with her more traditional journalist's tool kit to help repair the damage? Dialogue journalism was born as a process for convening and hosting journalism-supported conversations across social and political fault lines. "If what we're doing isn't working, if people don't trust us, if civil dialogue is contracting, how can we adapt our practices to better serve our highest calling, supporting our democracy?"

David Plazas says he returns again and again to a question he was asked at a Rotary Club event in 2018. "Why should I trust you?" a man in the audience asked. That question led Plazas, the opinion and engagement director for USA TODAY Network–Tennessee, to grapple with the uncomfortable impressions some of his rural neighbors had about "media elites" who looked down on them. Plazas describes his efforts to truly examine that critique and respond by leading changes that included a Civility Tennessee initiative, a podcast (*Tennessee Voices*), and the publication of two newsletters (*Black Tennessee Voices* and *Latino Tennessee Voices*) that try to shift from "telling stories *about*" people in these traditionally underrepresented communities to "telling stories *for* and *with* them." These and other efforts are aimed at connecting with people in the communities his news organization serves. "This is about meaningful and intentional public service for our fellow citizens in order to help preserve and strengthen our democratic republic."

Linda Miller began collaborating with Kettering when, after leading the groundbreaking Public Insight Network (PIN) at Minnesota Public Radio, she was encouraging journalists to deepen their relationships with residents and advocate for the community. She now leads the Multicultural Media and Correspondents Association's Equitable Media and Economies Initiative. In her essay, Miller explores what it might mean to adopt an ethic of care in journalism. While it's acceptable for journalists to care about seeking the truth about the *issues* they write about, she says that openly caring about the *people* they write about is often thought to interfere with news judgment. "Yet," she writes, "if journalists cannot advocate for their communities' well-being, what, exactly, is their purpose?"

In his role as cofounder of City Bureau and codirector of national impact, Darryl Holliday, a former beat reporter and photojournalist, is leading a movement to update the way we visualize democracy. He begins with the proposition that, for the most part, the professional media workforce—"disproportionately White, male, able-bodied, and cis" and "significantly more wealthy, educated, and politically left" than those in the communities they serve—cannot fully reflect those communities. One way to remedy the situation, he says, is through expanding the ranks of those who produce journalism, "not just as news consumers, but as distributors and—most important—producers of local information." The process is already underway in the form of new, participatory media organizations, such as his own City Bureau, a civic journalism lab cultivating the information and storytelling networks that democratize access to civic power. "Our vision for the future of local news . . . reframes the traditional consumer-producer relationship into one of cocreation, with journalists and communities working together to produce essential public goods."

These essays are just a sampling of the innovations afoot in journalism and provide a peek into the kind of behind-the-scenes introspection about craft that the public rarely sees. We hope you will enjoy getting to know these journalists in their own words. By providing this deeper look at the care with which they, and thousands like them, approach their work, we also hope to add dimension to the public's view of journalism.

As editors partnering with these gifted writers, we were reminded that writing is, itself, a process of learning. Writing is a disciplined form of thinking that requires assessment, reflection, and revisions that hone understanding. As Joan Didion famously said, "I write entirely to find out what I'm thinking, what I'm looking at, what I see and what it means." These authors dug deep into themselves and their experiences to add to our understanding of democracy and to help us understand the different ways that journalism is being reinvented to strengthen it. We are grateful they did.

Reorienting Journalism to Favor Democratic Agency

by Subramaniam Vincent

There is a politics that drives journalistic decision-making. It is deeply layered and implicit. It is journalistic culture. This politics underlies the implicit and explicit exercise of journalistic power behind the scenes: How and when does a development become newsworthy? What represents fact and what represents a *claim*? Which facts and claims are elevated, and which ones are not? Which narratives are pushed, and which are sidelined? Whose perspectives are centered, and whose are not? Whose frames are adopted, and whose are not? Whose lived experiences count, and whose do not? Which cultural threats are exposed and labeled, and which ones are ignored? Who is quoted at length and extensively, and who is paraphrased? When does the headline match the story in the body, and when does it spin misinformation? When must a piece be labeled opinion, and when not? Whose stock pictures are depicted when reporting about a profession, and whose are not?

American journalism, with its storied journey from the penny press to the partisan press to the news media of today, has seen disputes galore over its practices. And yet, by the 1960s, mainstream journalistic culture (both left and right) settled into what Matthew Pressman terms the "liberal values" of investigations, interpretation, adversarialism, and questioning authority.[1] One would think that, settled into these values and buttressed by a swath of legal protections under the First Amendment, mainstream journalism had met its sweet spot in liberal democracy.

Not so. Twenty years after the turn of the century, journalism is under siege in many of the very democracies that were its acclaimed protectors. The siege is not merely economic. It is cultural. Journalistic culture is under attack on multiple fronts. In the United States, it manifests in journalism's inability to help move the public to judgment on some of the greatest questions a country might face.

A reconstitution of the practice that we normatively call journalism today, so that it better serves democracy, is not going to come from economic salvation. It is more likely to come from a cultural transformation of the practice itself. Indeed, the cultural transformation may open the doors to new economic possibilities and that might in turn call for new economic investments. This essay will first outline a brief historical account connecting the evolution of journalism and democracy and the normative basis for the former's role in bolstering the latter. I will then detail the structural weaknesses in journalism that impede the advancement of democratic prospects and then move to recommendations for changes that may help journalism serve democracy more directly and intentionally.

Context and Connections: Democracy and Journalism

In the everyday rhetoric of modern democracy, the role of the free press is seen as essential. Essential to providing people with verified facts and stories. Essential to shining light on the truth. Everyone, from politicians, lawyers, and editors to scientists, jurists, and historians, connects the press and democracy both implicitly and explicitly.

Some people say the press is the immune system of democracy. The rhetoric connecting journalism and democracy is both evidence based and aspirational. It warrants elucidation because it will help expose structural weaknesses in journalism that have shackled its prospects for bolstering democracy.

A reconstitution. . . is more likely to come from a cultural transformation of the practice itself.

We must start with the word *democracy*. Its original meaning has been lost through the emergence of modern nation-states. In common parlance, people lean toward a meaning of "majority rule" by "balloting" or "elections." A common misunderstanding is that it means everyone is entitled to an opinion, placing the thrust of the meaning on a speech plane. Others focus on a "rule of law" frame. But in his brief but insightful paper on the original meaning of the word *democracy*, political scientist Josiah Ober traces the roots of the word to the Greek *demos* (people) and *kratos* (power). Ober writes that democracy did not mean just the "power of the demos . . . relative to other potential power-holders in the state." He traces ancient Greek literature and deduces that *kratos* originally referred to a (newly) activated political capacity; *democracy* refers to the collective capacity of a *demos* to do things in the public realm. And this includes the "collective strength and ability to act within that realm and, indeed, to reconstitute the public realm through action."[2]

This is agency.

Liberal democracy came about because of the need to enshrine and commit to law a set of inalienable rights for all citizens that their nations and states could not curtail or clip. Breaking unjust social hierarchies required not only the kindled *agency* of marginalized people, but also a regime of rights to translate that agency into real power and to justify it through a process of reasoned speech. Human rights allow the protection and *expression* of that power and limit the state's inherent ability to bat it down. Without human rights, the agency of citizens to bring about equality and remove injustices does not become a long-term capacity and therefore power.

The evolution of liberal democracy became intertwined with the evolution of journalism around three ideas: truth, public reason, and multiculturalism. Liberal democracy elevated the importance of truth in the running of public affairs and decision-making. Historian Sophia Rosenfeld documents the contentious relationship between democracy and truth in her recent book, *Democracy and Truth: A Short History.* "Where monarchies were characterized by deception, lies, and hidden information . . . democracies would be committed to sincerity, to transparency; to accuracy and one of the things promised was that . . . truth would be the foundation on which policy got made but also a kind of product of democracies. Something like an aspiration," she says.[3]

Liberal democracy continues to this day to advance deliberation and public reason as its everyday work. Nobel laureate Amartya Sen calls this "government by discussion."[4] In his book *The Idea of Justice,* Sen echoes Ober in defining democracy around the "capacity to act" or "agency." For Sen, the central issues in a broader understanding of democracy are political participation, dialogue, and public interaction, all of which are really avenues for citizens to enact their agency and realize it as power. Sen notes that democracy is no longer seen just in terms of the demands for public balloting, "but much more capaciously, in terms of what John Rawls calls 'the exercise of public reason.'"[5]

Sen not only connects the concepts of democracy, public reason, and justice, but he also assigns to the press the responsibility for advancing public reasoning in a liberal democracy. He notes public reasoning is "constitutively related to the idea of democracy" and at the same time is crucial to "help assess the demands of justice."[6] He argues that a "well-functioning" media can play a critically important role in facilitating public reasoning in general and hence enable the public pursuit of justice.

To situate Sen's use of the normative term *well-functioning* for media, it is helpful to look to Jürgen Habermas', two-fold structure: a) the "public sphere" abstraction and b) the mass media's capacity to focus public attention. Habermas posits the idealized public sphere as the domain of social life where public opinions are formed. It is here that the communication and attention needed for reasoning occurs, competing opinions are aired, and support for public will is formed—all of which are needed to legitimize democratic political rule.[7] He also argues that a mass media-controlled public sphere has the capacity to focus the attention of the public on key issues. Public attention becomes easier to build on issues, such as social justice, health care, taxation, a pandemic, schooling, or housing, that relate to the lived experiences and aspirations of people and communities.

But issues can be controversial, especially if competing values are in conflict or if the facts themselves are in dispute. Controversies draw public attention. Like conflict, drama, and bad news, controversy itself is a news value. Controversies draw journalists in and inevitably occupy considerable space and time in the media. But controversies can be stoked by elite powers exploiting their relationships with journalists. Hence, what constitutes a controversy for journalism is itself a key ethical question because once a journalist has determined that an issue is controversial, the principle of fairness (or impartiality) in reporting requires citing multiple viewpoints rooted in facts and evidence. The determination of a topic as controversial by news organizations is a conscious gatekeeping decision and has always played a key role in catalyzing public attention.[8]

A systematic way to think about journalistic behavior around controversy is offered by the journalism historian Daniel Hallin in his book on media coverage of the Vietnam War.[9] Hallin's idea conceptualizes boundaries between controversies that are legitimate and those that aren't. He introduces the three regions as concentric spheres: consensus, legitimate controversy, and deviance. Hallin offers this model to explain why and when journalists tend to present opposing views (both-sideism) or adopt a more disinterested or "objective" approach to a topic. It is important to note that while Hallin offered a model describing how journalists operate, he did not offer an ethical principle to determine the legitimacy of controversies themselves. This is needed to help decide when to air multiple competing sides and when not.[10] This is particularly important in the present day since social media platforms give political elites the ability to stoke arbitrary and illegitimate controversies merely by uttering false and incendiary statements about the "other" group and letting them spread. Determining a controversy's legitimacy before reporting not only lets the press contribute in principle to the formation of competing public opinions, but it also allows the mass media to help focus public attention on which controversies and problems are more pressing *now* and which are not.

But how does a public come to judgment on a key question? Daniel Yankelovich proposes a model for how Americans move from initial opinions to *public judgment*. He articulates a three-stage process in "The Bumpy Road from Mass Opinion to Public Judgment":[11]

Consciousness raising. "Consciousness raising is the stage in which the public learns about an issue and becomes aware of its existence and meaning," Yankelovich says. Journalists readily recognize that this is a key role they play.

Working through. Working through issues starts when people are confronted with the need to make change and become actively involved and engaged with each other. Then they must "confront the cross pressures that ensnare them." This takes time and has ups and downs. "There is a wrenching discontinuity between consciousness raising and working through that is a major source of difficulty in any effort to improve the quality of public opinion," writes Yankelovich, noting that our institutions are typically weaker at helping people work through well and speedily.

Resolution. This is usually multifaceted and typically the result of the first two stages during which people, having had their consciousness raised and worked through the issues, have resolved where they cognitively, emotionally, and morally stand. Hence, there is a public judgment as opposed to mass opinion.

"Public judgment is different from expert knowledge and implies a civic process of coming together across differences," Yankelovich says. His statement finds echoes in Rosenfeld's view on shared realities emerging from a balance between experts' truths and ordinary people's truths. Talking about the relationship between democracy and truth, Rosenfeld says that what evolved as democracy was that no one person, no one institution, no one method was going to be given a monopoly on determining what the truth was. The truth was going to be a collective product and worked out in a messy way among ordinary people, their representatives, and experts in and out of government. "This left truth always being both highly regarded as an aspiration and messy and often really contentious. People have fought over who gets to say what's true and how they determine what that is, as well as what truth consists of ever since," Rosenfeld says. People's take on what's true and experts' take on what's true have always been in some tension, though they are supposed to balance each other, she points out.[12]

With this as a backdrop, the next section will throw light on multiple structural weaknesses in journalism that hurt the advancement of democratic prospects even in nations where a "free press" already operates. We look at journalistic routines and processes as a system that has antidemocratic tendencies both within and outside newsrooms.

Journalism's Limited Immunity to Elitism and Hegemony

Journalism's powerful institutional position in the liberal democratic arena has not meant that news organizations themselves are democratic in culture. They did not in one fell swoop embrace the spirit of human rights and dignity for all people and translate this into determinations of newsworthiness, news selection, sourcing, and crafting stories on issues impacting marginalized communities.

Elitism has always been an ethical weakness in journalism, in particular for breaking news stories. Journalists want people to know what experts and those in positions of structural power are thinking. A controversy may arise, a scam may be unfolding, there might have been a firing or a resignation, and so forth. Journalists want the public to know that they spoke to people in positions of authority, and they see this as important to the perceived credibility of their story. All this is to say that it puts journalism in proximity to elite power and official authority and at a relative distance from the democratic agency of the people. The latter, which often springs up and lives in grassroots efforts, groups, and movements, has for too long been dismissed as "activism." Yet, members of grassroots groups often have an altogether different experience with the problem from that of people in positions of power. As a result, their ideas for solutions are also unique.

> Elitism in journalism has also let officials cause cultural harm by criminalizing entire communities and ethnic groups.

Journalists lean toward quoting people in positions of formal authority and power rather than ordinary people. The reasons range from mainstream news values (conflict, controversy, drama, outrage, bad news, good news, disorder, solutions)[13] to the need for a story to be credible and to the desire to spread knowledge by questioning and interpreting officials on behalf of the public. Experts (knowledge authorities), officials (governmental or political authorities), civil society actors, and officeholders wielding some type of structural power in their communities (organizations, networks, and institutions) are the ones most likely to shape the frame of the story and be quoted in it. Elitism in journalism has also let officials cause cultural harm by criminalizing entire communities and ethnic groups.

This leaning of journalism toward elite power implicitly compromises its own truth-determination process, especially on issues about which there is a cultural divide or division of opinion along social, cultural, or class lines. Elitism causes newsrooms to disregard the struggles and aspirations of working-class people and the truths they live and experience. Working-class people include large numbers of White Americans. Journalism academic Christopher Martin documents this multidecade trend in his aptly titled book, *No Longer Newsworthy: How the News Media Abandoned the Working Class*.[14] Martin documents four decades of journalism that deprioritized the American worker and framed him as a White male. He also records the disappearance of labor as a beat for newspaper reporters.

Rosenfeld's views about the tension between elite truths and ordinary people's truths have bearing here. "When they are in balance, early thinkers about democracy considered you might have something like a consensual low-lying level of *shared reality*; when they are out of whack, there was always going to be a danger."[15] This is a deeply understated insight about how shared realities may come about in a population. Since journalists are often talking to non-elite members of the public(s) as well as officials and experts with power, it seems to fall naturally to journalism to devise its truth-determination around both ordinary people's truths and experts' truths. This means that reporters paint a more comprehensive and coherent picture in their stories by examining and drawing from both elite truths and ordinary people's truths. This also becomes a way to avoid simplistic narratives that one group or other may prefer, whereas the reality may be more complicated. But when elitism holds sway over journalistic routines and sensibilities, the media's ability to do this is subverted.

In examining the *New York Times*'s coverage of the North American Free Trade Agreement's (NAFTA's) signing in the 1990s, Christopher

Martin reveals the blind spots of American journalism when covering the working class:

> The *New York Times* failed to be a countervailing power (to use John Kenneth Galbraith's term)[16] for working people in 1992-93, precisely at the time when it was most needed, just as government (with majorities in both parties lined up in favor of NAFTA) had failed to be a countervailing power for working people. Government and the mainstream news media were in the corner of GM and other corporations. No one was in labor's corner.[17]

Martin's use of the words *countervailing power* in connection with the press has particular significance in our discussion of journalism and democracy because it is an assertion about journalistic power. It was and is a lost opportunity for the press to responsibly exercise its power. The disappearance of labor as a beat took away the ability of the press to set the agenda on labor issues outside of election time campaign bytes. It also coincided with the ascendance of the neoliberal consensus in the United States between Republicans and Democrats in leadership beginning in the early 1990s. The neoliberal consensus itself was an elite consensus.

When we exclude entire communities, we exclude their truths and their agency to demand and bring change. It is not surprising that White working-class folks who felt alienated were also up for grabs when the evangelical right-wing agenda and Fox News started gaining ground in the 1990s with the launch of cable news. Equally, working-class issues cut across racial and gender lines. Black women factory workers lost their jobs in Rust Belt downsizing just as White men did. By dropping coverage, the opportunity for all working-class people to see themselves together (White, Black, people of color) in solidarity for a common cause against an extractive elite system was lost.

This is what makes journalism's role for and in democracy so critical. It is about both truth *and* power. Journalistic power when ethically used can legitimize the seeking of power by the non-elite. It helps people see their own agency and realize it as power in the public square. This itself is a democratizing influence journalism can have.

Mainline hegemony, the influence exerted by a dominant group (such as White culture in the US or Hindutva culture in India) while inhibiting alternative ideas and norms, is the second structural weakness in journalism. Support for the hegemonic group or culture is a root weakness in journalistic practice because it hurts the blossoming of democratic culture in multicultural societies in particular. Journalism at its core is a cultural occupation and, historically, has itself been practiced exclusively by the hegemonic group. This is why it has implicitly reproduced the perspectives of the dominant cultural groups at the cost of other groups, especially communities of color. The National Advisory Commission on Civil Disorders (the Kerner Commission), in its report of 1968, asked the American press to recognize the *existence* and activities of African Americans as part of the nation itself.[18]

In his book *White News*, Don Heider calls out White (and often male) hegemony in the American press, with people of color often framed as actors in traditional ethnic festivals or as deviant criminals. "Hegemony is evident in the practice of news decision-making that continually reinforces values and norms held by White managers who have no stake in radical change," writes Heider. Heider exposes how newsroom culture prevents the coverage of the truths that people of color experience and would like to see covered. Without self-reflection, the whole area of news judgment—determining what is news—is culturally self-validating.[19]

The same is true for much-needed investigative reporting on threats to democracy from nativism, White supremacy, and confederacy movements. After Charlottesville, where the White supremacist "Unite the Right" rally took place in 2017, there was a lone call by one journalist asking for White nationalism to be made into a beat in American newsrooms.[20] Since then, *Mother Jones* magazine has such a beat.[21] This reticence in journalism to examine domestic threats to democracy tracks with the Department of Homeland Security (DHS). It took until 2020 for DHS to classify White nationalism and supremacy as the highest domestic terror threat.[22] It has always been easier for the American intelligence establishment to name, target, and blacklist foreign organizations such as ISIS and al-Qaeda.

Domestic cultural conflict in multicultural societies is difficult to cover responsibly and in ways that promote mutual understanding. One of the better interviews after the Atlanta spa shootings of March 2021, when 21-year-old Robert Aaron Long killed six Asian women, was on Kara Swisher's *New York Times* podcast, *Sway*. Swisher talked with Korean American poet and award-winning author Cathy Park Hong. She asked Hong about how to change the discussions. And the poet said, "I think people don't know how to talk about interracial conflicts and misunderstandings or misperceptions. We haven't quite developed a vocabulary for it."[23] Hong also explained why she's seeking power, not assimilation, in conversations.

Hong tells Swisher that Asian Americans (still) live under the shadow of the model minority myth, which is used as proof that American exceptionalism and capitalism works for minorities. She refers to it as "this kind of contract where as long as we behave and keep quiet and so forth, we're fine." As an Asian American, she has seen that the benefit of assimilation is that you're left alone, she says. "However, it's not the same as having any kind of power."

Hong's aspiration in seeking power and a new vocabulary is reflected in the work of David McIvor and Michael Rios on how citizens avoid talking about power in conversations.[24] They cite Nina Eliasoph's remarkable observation about how discussions of power in everyday public conversations were frequently excluded by the boundaries of civic etiquette—the norms and codes of speech that shape interactions within civic life. Eliasoph said that in a democracy people create the public by talking, and the modes and content of public conversation will therefore dramatically affect citizens' sense of agency or efficacy. Citizens seem uncomfortable with discussions of power, but it may be precisely these discussions that make possible the actualization of their power, write Rios and McIvor.

Kettering Foundation Program Officer Derek Barker writes that given multiculturalism, "forging trust across divides of race, class, and culture is a matter of collectively developing habits and skills of public reason." But echoing Hong's comment on not wanting to assimilate, Barker maintains:

> This does not mean that minorities ought to simply assimilate their perspectives into that of a homogeneous public. Rather, perhaps the most pressing task for realizing a deliberative democracy is for majorities to better understand the distinct and legitimate perspectives of minorities.[25]

This is really why journalism's growth in hegemonic soil is antidemocratic. Hegemony is the cultural barrier to expanding understanding and is often invisible until called out. In order for journalism to foster multicultural conversations about power that could foster mutual understanding, journalistic culture needs to be transplanted from its default hegemonic habitat into democratic soil.

Elitism and hegemony in newsrooms have allowed public reason to develop and become catalytic to decision-making only in select areas where White-led institutions—government and civil society—invited it. On many long-running public questions (for example, reparations for Black Americans), White media do not play a role in encouraging public reason to develop through deliberation around historical facts and human rights conventions.

Mainstream news values are shortcuts that allow editors and reporters to exercise news judgment and determine newsworthiness quickly and in a way that is professionally accepted in other newsrooms. Scholars Tony Harcup and Deirdre O'Neill cataloged a list of mainline news values such as conflict, disorder, bad news, drama, celebrity, controversy, good news, and disasters.[26] The acceptance of these values is implicit and manifests in multiple news organizations reporting the same larger story after the first outlet has broken the initial report.

These news values are not evaluated around their inherent worth for deepening democracy. By their very nature, claims or developments or events that meet the newsworthiness test under these news values do not sufficiently resolve whether there is a contestation of factual narratives or ideas or policies in a democracy (expected and legitimate) or a contestation over liberal democracy and its own ends. Reporters must cover the latter type of contest, too, but they must call out to the public that it is the latter type. Sourcing and framing of claims and discontent cannot operate as if it were the former type of contest. Otherwise, journalists may equate antidemocratic actors with democratic ones and harm democratic agency. A second problem is that these news values give extremely limited latitude for spotting and developing stories about diverse communities in conflicts discussing power in a multicultural sphere as democratic equals.

Such discussions can easily take on a controversial air, but unless journalists are willing to slow down and not turn every controversy into a reporting opportunity, the skills of having such conversations themselves in public and expanding the range of civic etiquette (as we noted earlier) will not come about.

> Social media design also privileges affective communication around emotions and feelings, and drives fast thinking.

Social media's anti-deliberative design challenges journalism. Independent of elitism and hegemony as internal threats, a challenging complication in the relationship between journalism and democracy coming from the outside is social media. Social media and search platforms are primarily advertising businesses. Advertising businesses, just like the mass media, are attention based. But there is a far deeper granularity with which social media, using algorithmic newsfeeds and advertisement targeting technology, can personalize content and social experiences. The supply of content is infinite, but our attention is finite and comes at a premium. The term *attention economy* is used to describe the connection between content, people, and platforms.

As products, social media platforms make a lot of tall claims about speech and connecting people. But they mostly facilitate asynchronous speech—that is, you and I and millions of others can say what we want to say to anyone else without worrying about being countered in real time. This type of speech does not itself create a public. For deliberative conversations to proceed, a synchronous setup such as a debate or dialogue is better suited because *speech and counterspeech are exchanged in real time.* When moderated by journalists who are committed to inserting facts and historical context, a democratic public can emerge. Social media design, be it Twitter or Facebook or YouTube, privileges asynchronous speech. Deliberative conversations on social media are possible, but they need substantially more moderation effort and self-restraint.

Social media design also privileges affective communication around emotions and feelings, and drives fast thinking. Daniel Kahneman, in his seminal book, *Thinking, Fast and Slow*, lays out an accessible foundation for understanding the human brain's vulnerabilities. His insights have deep significance in the digital media era and therefore implications for public reason and judgment.

The brain is "a machine for jumping to conclusions," writes Kahneman. He describes our brains operating in two systems each influencing the other. System 1 is the faster, emotional, instinctive, and intuitive brain. System 2 is the slower, lazier, but more deliberate and reasoning brain. When looking at belief, Kahneman draws on the work of psychologist Daniel Gilbert, pointing out that "even nonsensical statements evoke initial belief." Gilbert proposes in his essay "How Mental Systems Believe" that "understanding a statement must begin with an attempt to believe it: you must first know what the idea would mean if it were true. Only then can you decide whether or not to unbelieve it."[27] Kahneman extends that argument to show that the initial attempt to believe is System 1 in action. System 2 of our brain is needed to undo it. System 1 does not keep alternatives for critical or deliberate comparison; System 2 does. But if System 2 is busy, System 1 will jump to conclusions.[28]

System 1 uses associative memory whose operations contribute to general confirmation bias, notes Kahneman. "The confirmation bias of System 1 favors *uncritical* acceptance of suggestions and exaggeration of the likelihood of extreme and improbable events. System 2 is in charge of doubting and unbelieving, but it can be busy; it is lazier and requires more effort." And even System 2, when it comes into play, "makes a deliberate search for confirming evidence to test a hypothesis."

In another seminal book, *Behave: The Biology of Humans at Our Best and Worst*, Robert Sapolsky explains how the activation of the amygdala—a tiny, almond-shaped part of our brain—during fearmongering, for instance, almost instantly returns our brain to the many older "us vs. them" dichotomies of race and tribe.

With social media and massive information overload, reasoning together with "others" is even more difficult because of ongoing polarization and how easy it is to foster tribalistic (anti-deliberative) conversations. The primary means of joining these conversations— likes, shares, retweets, and forwards—allow the public to participate in spreading behaviors with enhanced virality and without regard for accuracy. Its frictionless design (which serves advertising business models) puts us into "fast thinking" mode.

So, social media, hugely successful at fostering conversation at one level, are nevertheless inherently anti-deliberative in design. Leaders can campaign with hundreds and thousands of online groups during an election race as legitimate political activity. Antidemocratic political parties and campaigners can gain popular support. Illiberal and pseudoscientific forces have been able to organize and strike ever more powerfully against the truth and justice-seeking forces (whom liberal democracy favors) than they could before. Social media give antidemocratic actors equal opportunity and power to balkanize public attention and public reason around controversial topics.[29]

Public attention has been usurped by the gaming of individual attention at the consumer-click level.

Public attention has been usurped by the gaming of individual attention at the consumer-click level, which leads to participatory narratives that draw people into partisan factions and onwards into confusion, mistrust, and conspiracies about "the others." In sum, bad actors are able to attack, disrupt, and derail the already imperfect, slow, and discursive process of public reason, truth-determination, and judgment.

All of this erodes journalism's normative power to focus public attention on issues and allow competing public opinions and judgment to develop in the media. The determination of legitimate controversies becomes harder in the race to grab morsels of attention. Journalism is not going to sit on the sidelines while social media platforms, as noted earlier, give political elites the ability to stoke arbitrary and illegitimate controversies merely by uttering false and incendiary statements about the "other" group and letting them spread. Once these controversies are lit up on social media, journalists do not want to be left behind in their search for relevant stories to tell. They enter the fray in the name of trending topics as a proxy to newsworthiness, and very quickly, multiple views—those based on facts and those based on lies and disinformation—all make their way into press coverage, leading to even greater amplification.

For instance, during the run-up to the 2020 US presidential election, mainstream news outlets that also had major presence and play on social media were amplifying President Donald Trump's preemptive and strategically calculated claims of massive prospective mail-in ballot fraud. They were initially covered by large sections of the mainstream press, including television networks, as if this were a legitimate controversy until August when more of them started labeling those views as lies and false claims.[30] Journalism thus initially allowed an illegitimate controversy to be legitimized even though, eventually, the mainstream media did change course. The news organizations still treated everything the then-president and his influential supporters said as newsworthy, even as they carried rebuttals by others. The oldest newsworthiness rule—what the president says is newsworthy, without qualification—turned out to be a key antidemocratic weakness within the traditional journalistic media. Even debunking is not a magic bullet because it can end up elevating the original misinformation even further.

Reporters constantly use social media trends to determine "news" and sometimes end up amplifying a disinformation narrative unwittingly by calling attention to it—without realizing the power their own social media accounts have.

Furthermore, adversarial journalism—in which reporters treat politicians as adversaries and question them—is easy to take out of context on social media. It hurts deliberation. Deliberation is a way for public reason to emerge as discursive communities work through an issue that has gained widespread attention. Deliberation is different from debate, which has an inevitable win-lose scenario to reckon with. Debates also tend to drive adversarial behavior and in turn engender the same in follower communities. Deliberation needs to be supported affirmatively and fostered intentionally. But unreason and reason now compete for opinion formation directly on social media, with journalistic media trying to keep pace. The public reason we want requires slower thinking and deliberation in humanized settings. Interactions on social media over political issues are largely fast thinking based, and people tend to double down on their positions. Such interactions do not support sound, thoughtful, or careful judgment. Political philosopher Hannah Arendt's views on lies in politics seem prophetic when read today:

> If everybody always lies to you, the consequence is not that you believe the lies, but rather that nobody believes anything any longer. . . . And a people that no longer can believe anything cannot make up its mind. It is deprived not only of its capacity to act but also of its capacity to think and to judge. And with such a people you can then do what you please.[31]

Recommendations

With elitism and hegemony already shackling journalism, social media's anti-deliberative design further constrains journalism's potential to serve the public by gaining its attention, slowing down its thinking, and helping it arrive at public judgment.

The leverage the mass media once had on the public sphere has more or less disintegrated, or is disintegrating.[32] What follows are some recommendations for how journalism might reclaim its democratic potential.

Reconstitute journalism with a prodemocracy bias. Every day journalists must settle on a meaning for the word *democracy*. It must go beyond such procedure-based references as elections, equal political parties, majority rule, rule of law, peaceful transfer of power, coequal branches of government, and anticorruption investigations. Journalism must prioritize the meaning of *democratic agency*: the capacity of people to bring about change toward justice and equity using truths and facts. This capacity must be made visible in stories. People include communities, especially those socially and economically marginalized, and experts. Journalists must recognize that people or structures with more power are able to deploy their agency to greater ends than people with agency but less or no power. So, as part of their inclusion of experts *and* people, advancing democracy warrants that they look for unrecognized agency and that is seeking realization as power.

All values that journalists assert as core to their work are not equal. Newsrooms must draw up a hierarchy of values, but this is no easy task. Newsrooms must recognize or draw up a hierarchy of values. When values compete with each other, an intentional hierarchy helps resolve the dispute in favor of the higher value, instead of arbitrarily trading off one value for another. Dignity, equality, fairness, justice, and anticorruption, for example, are apex values. What signals an apex value is that it is most often used in an absolute sense: dignity and equality *for all* human beings. Neutrality (or impartiality), and balance, on the other hand, are not apex values. They are below apex values. We could call them "middle values" in democratic significance. The signal of a middle value is that it is usually qualified one way or another to understand its ethical use. Neutrality toward whom? Neutrality to what end? These questions must be answered on democratic grounds before journalism can determine sourcing, which in turn helps journalists frame the stories around the perspectives and views of people. And the decision to be neutral has to be made *after* the determination on the legitimacy of a controversy is done.

Another example of a middle journalistic value is "the public needs to know this now." Breaking news journalists often assert that merely because a high political actor—to whom they have accorded newsworthiness—has said something, they are responsible in ensuring that the public learns it right away as opposed to applying a speed bump to minimize harm. People in power know how to exploit neutrality and frame false or misleading narratives. Antidemocratic actors use these tactics well to sow confusion, fear, and long-term anxiety in exchange for giving access to journalists. Journalists must openly call out antidemocracy actors instead of treating them as "legitimate" voices.

Journalistic discussions of accuracy have a tendency to back themselves into the defensible arena of facts and fact-checking. But facts are too atomistic to be useful in and of themselves. Human lives are like quilts, complex fabrics with tapestry and texture, often painfully pieced together by the people who live them. Even in nature, atoms make up molecules, which make up crystals, polymers, and all sorts of real and complex formations. Fact-checking is necessary and yet never sufficient. A factual story around a freeway project about to dissect working-class or Black neighborhoods can be written with little representation of perspectives of the impacted people. The story will be "factual"; that is, it will report what has happened in the development of the project and recent decisions taken. But the story may not be accurate.

Centering the story on the perspectives and lived experiences of impacted communities and including the historical context complicates the simplistic narrative.[33] But it lets the whole story, depicting multiple realities, come out. That in turn allows people with less power to become visible as people with agency make their legitimate claim for greater say over decisions that impact them. Accurate representations of stakeholders in a story require a determination of stakes and power, and these considerations drive a more inclusive gathering of views and otherwise neglected facts.

Beyond the immediate facts of any developing story, real stories are very often about the power that communities are seeking without saying so. The primary battles in the public sphere are often about stakes: Whose stakes matter more than others? Are there historical or recent trends of exclusion? Simply changing the vocabulary used in questions from factual alone (Did this happen? Do you deny this? What is your take?) or emotional (How do you feel about this?) to questions about power (Do you feel these rules give you enough power to weigh in? Whose stakes are higher than yours in this conflict?) can open up the conversation. More often than not, this will allow people to share their experiences in new and authentic ways around their needs. Journalism's promise to liberal democracy must be that it offers paths to help economically and socially marginalized people transform their agency into real power and in that sense make democracy real for everyone, not just the social and economic elite.

Professional news organizations have to make open declarations of their news values together. At the current moment, very few news organizations (barring mission-driven ones) have a page on their websites disclosing what their news values are and how their values relate to determining newsworthiness. Moving to a disclosure-based approach will make it easier for democratic reform efforts in journalism to then ask for new news values. Making open declarations will also let the public(s) have the opportunity to see news values called out explicitly and have an opportunity to respond.

> Win-win solutions that disparate communities have found through dialogue and deliberation need to be elevated.

When communities reach resolution through deliberation, as opposed to being locked in bitter conflict, that needs to be a news value in its own right and drive journalistic agendas. Stories highlighting rights conflicts in the higher courts often give the impression that in a rule-of-law society, disputes are settled win-lose only in the judiciary.[34] They tend to get framed along a binary "your right vs. my right" setup. Conflict, as we noted earlier, is a news value and drives stories. But conflict stories need not be win-lose alone. Win-win solutions that disparate communities have found through dialogue and deliberation need to be elevated through stories above the incessant flow of "win-lose" news about groups fighting litigations in the courts.

This is really an untapped opportunity for journalism since its forum function is a natural fit for citizens in conversation with each other, both in stories and events. Journalistic coverage can advance public understanding and allow the development of vocabulary to help the public discuss complex cultural and political concerns, including power itself, across racial and ethnic identities. It can help the public discuss cultural conflict without diminishing the agency of people of color or making ordinary White Americans with no ties to White nationalist groups feel like they are always about to trip over themselves in a conversation or just be seen as the enemies of democracy.

Local histories that provide a more accurate picture of what a community has had to experience has to be a news value so that breaking news and enterprise stories that are accompanied by historical context illuminate dark systemic patterns on an ongoing basis. A society's capacity to judge and support policy is also based on its memory and accounting of past injustices in full. Katherine Franke, a historian and law scholar at Columbia University, pointed out that the case for reparations for African Americans was clearly made as early as 1861 after the emancipation proclamation.[35] Entire generations of Americans have grown up (and are admitting to this now) without learning about the massacres of Black people between the end of Reconstruction in the 1870s and the passage of the Voting Rights Act in 1965. This is erasure of collective memory among privileged and underprivileged communities. But the privileged have more power. So, the cost to democracy in terms of the accompanying empathy and solidarity deficits is higher when they do not have this memory.

Slow journalism down. The genre of journalism that has the greatest risk of conflict with democracy in the social media era is breaking news. The routine "get-the-facts-and-publish" machine operates as if journalism were still running in the pre-social media era. Then, the press was the gatekeeper, narrative setter, and the news experience giver, and the distributor; this is no longer true. Journalism of that era was a force for both good and bad. Breaking news often justifies its publishing decisions on the grounds that "the public needs to know now." The need to know now is not a moral principle that trumps every other competing moral question, particularly the harm caused by amplifying misinformation, disinformation, hate, and fearmongering on social media. (Also see the part about apex values and middle values above.)

Breaking news about the mere utterances of politicians accusing each other of something or other cannot compete with social media where the same public figures already talk directly to their own followers and say everything they want, discredit anyone, or simply sow confusion and doubt. A famous Tamil hip-hop song from the movie *Thani Oruvan* has a line that says, "Only for truth to win, you need evidence; for lies to win, confusion is enough." Social media have created a culture around user-generated content (UGC). UGC posts do not intrinsically require truths or fact-based realities for communications to proceed. Restricting breaking news to the painstaking work where reporters excavate authentic realities that social media simply cannot offer or compete with in its own UGC experiences is a long overdue reprioritization.

Social psychology and neuroscience have illuminated how the brain works in ways that are being used for decision-making analysis in many areas such as conflict resolution, mediation, and management. Antidemocratic actors already know that the best way to blind people to truth and evidence is to trigger tribal divisions in the mind around "others"—people of other races genders, castes, or classes. The human brain is not neutral to all information thrown at it. If the headlines of stories and rhetorical statements made in political speech are deliberately framed to trigger particular values, or pull up a narrative that we already feel we belong in, or elevate a skepticism we share, then that pathway becomes a filter. It will accept facts and evidence that fit and reject the ones that don't. Group identity and loyalties can complicate this further. In practical terms, slowing journalism down will allow journalists to afford themselves the opportunity to critically examine the impressions that fleeting and episodic news coverage may leave on different communities involved. Since journalists are most concerned with releasing facts and information to the public, journalism education programs would do well to synthesize the best knowledge from the cognitive sciences today. If journalistic actors are to align with democracy, they must receive training on how bad actors can exploit the weakness of mental pathways to marginalize the possibility of civic deliberation and judgment.

Distinguish between news and journalism. Clarifying the difference between news and journalism will make it easier for the latter to help democracy. Everyone—every group, every momentarily put-together network—has a voice and can join or create false or true narratives about any other person or group. A million sites may exist online, all claiming to be news. But which ones do responsible journalism? Not every initiative claiming to be news can claim to be doing journalism. News is not journalism. News is the product. Journalism is a process. And yet the distinction is rarely pointed out or justified by news organizations themselves. Making and discussing the distinction has many benefits.

First, it will make it easier to separate responsible journalism from its cavalier forms. The normative aspects of journalism, such as the slower truth-determination function, its ethics, including anti-elitism, anti-racism, diversity, and inclusion, must be more visible and accessible in the everyday vocabulary of public discussion. Otherwise, the public will not believe prodemocracy norms even exist in journalism. In turn, this will help cocreate new practices with the public engaged in an issue. It will mitigate against the simplistic narratives around media bias in today's partisan cultural context, where accusations— both rightfully and wrongfully—are hurled at journalists. Defending a bias in favor of democracy becomes easier and brings nuance into the otherwise emotional conversations.

Second, social media platforms need to be open to designing their technology systems to parse journalistic behavior and not just news content, fact-checking, clickbait tracking, and reputation signals. Making distinctions between journalism and news will make it easier for social media organizations to classify news sites that do journalism from news sites that don't. That in itself will help elevate truth-determination in democracy.

Journalism: Evolving with the People

by Doug Oplinger

While visiting with a friend and mentor a few years ago, we wondered whether our craft of journalism could recover its place in democracy. "Recover" assumed that it in fact had a place. We believed that it did—three, four, and five decades ago—because at that time, there was a tangible reaction to our reporting. But as the information ecosystem changed at an accelerating and convulsive rate in the age of the internet—as did American culture—journalism practices failed to keep pace and mainstream media's resonance diminished. Newsrooms continued to methodically cover beats, produce story leads with binary tension, expound on data that spelled doom, and adhere to conventional rules of practice. Too many journalists were deaf to clamors from increasingly distressed communities where people were saying that journalists were harming rather than facilitating their participation in democracy.

Our musings led my friend, David Holwerk, to offer up the best shock-value headline his former editorial page editor skills could muster: "The worst thing to ever happen to journalism was an ethics code." The ethics code, he said, was designed in part so that journalists had a roadmap to accuracy, thoroughness, fairness, and objectivity. Nothing wrong with that concept, he argued, except that in practice, journalists used it to *not* be engaged personally in community life, or even feign to care, lest they jeopardize their nonexistent objectivity.

He kept going: The ethics code had become a shield behind which journalists hid. The separation from communities allowed too many journalists, if not entire newsrooms, to lose a feeling of responsibility to the greater good. There was contempt toward a complex citizenry who defied simple story leads. Perhaps spoiled by decades of exorbitant profits and living in college-educated bubbles, newsrooms became aloof, if not arrogant. One might say we saw ourselves as a basket of non-deplorables.

I entered adolescence a few years before the fuzzy black and white televised images of John F. Kennedy's assassination and funeral redefined how we received breaking news. As a high school student in the 1960s, I had a perception of journalists as faceless White male stenographers feeding an information pipeline that emptied into every home, daily and on the hour. Some of my exceptions to the generic were a beloved Cleveland TV weatherman, a columnist in the local newspaper, and Walter Cronkite. Still, though, they were all White men. Newspapers were inexpensive, abundant, and thick; broadcast news, for the price of a radio or television, was free. I could find traditional news just as easily as turning on the water tap. For me, news was a commodity delivered by unseen people—and I took it for granted.

A career in journalism never crossed my mind. Who would want to be on the sidelines taking notes when there was an urgent need for people to carry the ball or call the plays? Afterall, I had ambitions to be president. And besides, an *Akron Beacon Journal* sports editor once referred to my school—heavily populated with West Virginia transplants—in big headline type as full of "hicks." So much for liking newspeople. (Were we the '60s version of a "basket of deplorables"?)

Perhaps spoiled by decades of exorbitant profits and living in college-educated bubbles, newsrooms became aloof, if not arrogant.

I graduated from a transitioning rural-to-suburban school not far from Kent State University in the same month four students were killed there by Ohio National Guardsmen. I had a draft number of five and a student deferment from the military—that is, Vietnam—as long as I didn't fail my classes at the University of Akron. Everything in the news was relevant to me and every friend, cousin, and classmate. And yet I still saw journalists as on the sidelines.

Only months after graduating from high school, however, the vital role of journalism in democracy became so vivid that it still stirs deep emotion. To launch the career I sought in government service, I began attending local school board and township trustee meetings at age 18, often sitting in the front and asking questions. After one of those meetings, *Akron Beacon Journal* reporter William Hershey introduced himself, explained the role of a stringer, and asked whether I'd be willing to faithfully attend these meetings and phone him afterward with notes so that he could write a story. A few months later, I called Hershey late at night to inform him that a divided school board had fired the longtime school district chief executive. The next afternoon, on an inside page, was a story on the firing, by William Hershey and Doug Oplinger. "Interesting," was my reaction.

A few weeks later, though, "interesting" became a religious conversion to journalism.

Hershey called to say he couldn't attend the next school board meeting, so it was up to me. I approached the meeting room, found the door locked, lights off, and a sign saying the session had been moved to the auditorium. "Why the move?" I thought. But a low rumble could be heard from the auditorium, and as I stepped through the door and saw hundreds of residents, the answer was clear. People had read the paper, shared with others, decided to take action, and here they were. I grabbed a folding chair and placed it on the floor between the school board and the audience so that I could see in all directions. It struck me that only the *Akron Beacon Journal* had covered the previous meeting and reported on the firing. That news story inspired people to take part in democracy at the most basic levels (and in the next election, the board was substantively changed).

After that meeting, Hershey invited me to the *Akron Beacon Journal* newsroom to meet editors, gave me a notebook, and asked me to cover meetings in a few more communities. He sat me down at a typewriter to explain how to write a news story. (Others taught me to swear.) By April, I was only 19 and still in my first year of college when state desk editor Patrick Englehart handed me a job application and said, "Fill this out. We hired you." That same month, Englehart and his team won a Pulitzer Prize for coverage of the Kent State shootings. Dropped into greatness, I was overwhelmed by these new coworkers who exuded passion through tobacco smoke and expletive-laced sentences.

A curiously revered boss named Jack often stopped by to chat with Englehart and his team. Jack took an interest in me, too, as I became the newspaper's only business reporter. Jack, by the way, was John S. Knight, emeritus editor, Pulitzer Prize winner, cofounder of Knight Newspapers, whose fortune helped fund the John S. and James L. Knight Foundation. A few years after he died, I became business editor and our team led his paper to another Pulitzer Prize.

What we didn't know at the time was that there was a fatal flaw in our perception of ourselves. We thought we were driving democratic action. The reality is that people will drive their own action, with or without us. Our best hope was to offer a roadmap. Perhaps Jack Knight understood that subtlety in 1969 when he said, "Thus we seek to bestir the people into an awareness of their own condition, provide inspiration for their thoughts and rouse them to pursue their true interests."

A Community Roused

Involvement in the community and listening to people around us are critical to knowing what will stir action. That was the case in a 1980s hostile takeover attempt of Akron's largest employer and one of the most generous corporate citizens, Goodyear Tire & Rubber Company. By that time, the business desk had grown from one reporter—me—to two editors and six reporters. A stock market wire story one evening said in the next to last paragraph that Goodyear stock was most active on the New York Stock Exchange on rumors that it was a takeover candidate. We made calls and could cobble together no more than four paragraphs. A news editor rejected the story as page-one worthy because it was about stocks, and people don't understand stocks.

Our business team saw something more to the story. We saw it as potentially causing upheaval in Akron, an attack on quality of life—and a mystery to boot. Tens of thousands of area residents had ties to Akron's robust tire industry as employees, retirees, or in related businesses. That's how we approached it for the next two months. We talked to people in barbershops and to Wall Street brokers. We offered narratives, revelations, and graphics that helped the city stay informed.

A few weeks into the coverage, the *Akron Beacon Journal* circulation director regaled our business news team with stories of newspaper delivery trucks rushed by people wanting the latest on Goodyear. For the first time in decades, bootstrappers were standing in the middle of busy streets selling papers at red lights. We were told by Goodyear that their New York lawyers, working from the Akron war room, were sending people to the street to grab copies of the *Akron Beacon Journal* because the newspaper often had information they did not. Like modern analytics, our sales reports and community reaction showed that people were reading and coalescing. People mailed rubber bands to the French billionaire trying to acquire Goodyear (we had reported that he hated rubber bands), purchased stock to try to drive up the price, chartered buses to Washington, erected signs in yards, and canceled accounts with the Merrill Lynch brokerage, which we reported was financing the hostile takeover.

A few months later, we were awarded the Pulitzer Prize for General News Reporting, and along with that came requests to speak. While I would be asked many good questions about the purpose of journalism, nothing provoked introspection more than a *Wall Street*

Journal reporter's column that said our Goodyear coverage was not worthy of a Pulitzer. The author said we were guilty of parochialism and boosterism. We had not committed quality journalism.

We looked at it differently. We had been empowering people, which I suppose the *Wall Street Journal* columnist might suggest was "boosting." But to make that statement robs citizens of *their* role. They were reacting to information that was trustworthy, actionable, and well written. However, they were the ones who talked among themselves and acted. Someone had to say, "Let's charter a bus and go to Washington," and then get it done. Someone had to erect a sign that said, "Buy Goodyear stock" and start a movement. The real work was occurring among the people.

Over the next few years, the public journalism movement and Knight Ridder CEO Jim Batten would poke the bears inhabiting newsrooms by suggesting that maybe we needed to shift our attention to citizens.

Building on Knight's statement that we are to "bestir the people," Batten told the company's newspaper leadership that we were to "inform, engage, and entertain." Most of that was easy. Everyone agreed that newsrooms inform every day, and writers were thrilled to hear that they could entertain, but engage? People's varied life experiences create complexity that is difficult to craft into a story lede. Informing and entertaining would be slowed by the tedium of the many different perspectives on storm runoff, potholes, urban crime, drugs, and putting prayer back in the schools.

I was intrigued by the engage idea—how would that look?—but I also believed that Batten was missing a fourth dynamic. For my local reporting team, I said our mission was to "inform, engage, entertain, and provoke toward constructive action." My idea of "provoke" was that, as a journalist working at the Knight brothers' hometown newspaper, we should be a catalyst that spurs Akron to action.

At Batten's urging, newspapers experimented with town meetings to listen and steer coverage of issues in ways that resonated with citizens.

The Power of Innovative Listening

I was fortunate that my newspaper believed in listening to the community. In 1989, the managing editor who led us through the Goodyear project exposed us to focus groups as a way to observe people as they exchanged ideas with one another in heartfelt conversation, telling stories that journalists wouldn't think to pursue. And in those days, we had money. We hired one of the best focus group facilitators in the country, Alice Rodgers, whose work portfolio included some of the most high-powered consumer products companies in the world. Our topic that year was families—how they were changing as Ohio transitioned from a stable, highly paid industrial state to a service economy. We traveled the state with Rodgers, listening raptly as she posed open-ended, nonthreatening questions that we thought, at first, were pretty lame. But the trust she built among strangers in two hours opened a window into Ohio that few journalists could have achieved. She impressed us with the power of this unusual interview format. Privately, we also wrestled with a world we discovered outside our college-educated, highly paid professional circle or sphere. Overwhelmed by stories of divorce, unwanted pregnancies, job losses, college debt, and inequality, some journalists called the project "families from hell." But more importantly, the time on the road with Rodgers offered a transformational moment: We learned that we really didn't know how these life challenges were affecting democratic participation and what people needed from us.

I was fortunate that my newspaper believed in listening to the community.

I was reminded of this a few years ago at a Between Coasts conference at Northwestern University's Medill School of Journalism. Freelance and full-time journalists representing major national media outlets gathered with reporters and editors from small towns across the Midwest. The midwestern journalists were critical of those who descended from the coasts onto their towns, particularly at election time, extracting stories about life at diners. The term used was "parachute journalism." A national story about Portsmouth, Ohio, an economically struggling Ohio River town and site of one of the original opioid pill mills, was an example. After the first national news outlet did a story of people struggling with addiction, living under bridges, or pushing carts through town, other national newsrooms followed for two years with similar stories, even though Portsmouth had introduced innovative addiction treatment and had begun to address the problem. But are local, college-educated journalists any different? Too often, they talk to a so-called expert about a problem, look at data, then drive to a neighborhood in search of an example. Is that not parachute journalism? How would the story have more resonance if it had originated with a neighborhood dialogue on what is needed to improve life?

This problem is ever present in the coverage of racial equity.

A few years after our experience with Ohio families, the nation watched a video of a Black man, Rodney King, beaten by four Los Angeles police officers. The officers on trial in 1992 were acquitted of charges that they had used excessive force, and cities across the country erupted in protest. Immediately, newsrooms held meetings to discuss how they would address race. Ours was no exception, except that we always were an exception. We had one of the most diverse newsrooms in the state and in Knight Ridder, and our publisher, John Dotson Jr., and managing editor, Jim Crutchfield, were both Black. The entire newsroom was invited to meet and talk about what we thought we knew about race and what we should do. It would be nearly five months before we would launch the first of five news packages that would take all of 1993 to produce and publish. Each package was produced by a carefully balanced team with an equal number of White and Black staffers; 30 would be involved over time.

Our research for each installment began with simultaneous Black and White focus groups designed by Rodgers and a series of other facilitators who assisted her. The purpose was to let people in our community guide us through their own experiences with race. Rodgers, who is White, facilitated a conversation of White people, and Black facilitators led Black dialogues. After about 90 minutes, the two groups were brought together to discuss what they had said about each other. Invariably, White people were anxious for more conversation after learning that Black people shared their values and concerns. Black people, meanwhile, often expressed gratitude for being heard, though respectfully asking the question, "Why wouldn't you expect us to have shared values?"

Journalists huddled in a room down the hall to observe the dialogues on closed-circuit TV. There were simple revelations that were highly instructive. For example, a White fire department officer said in his focus group that Black firefighters have a higher rate of absenteeism. The statement caused an unpleasant murmur among the journalists watching remotely. Afterward, he told us he was in charge of collecting attendance reports from each fire station, so he sees the numbers. He showed us. It was very clear: department records showed that White firefighters had a better attendance rate. Asked to talk with us about the reports, a senior Black firefighter told us that only White firefighters take attendance, and they routinely turn the other way for White friends. Our muted reaction, "Oh," didn't come close to representing the personal and professional introspection that followed. At that moment, some of us (Whites), particularly those who were data-driven journalists, were introduced to institutionalized racism. And the data we had come to trust was now suspect.

As the race series approached the one-year mark, the publisher and editor took a step that left traditional journalists in our newsroom wondering, "Can they do that?" The newspaper asked community residents if they'd sign a pledge to work on their understanding of race, and we established a foundation to continue race dialogues. We filled page after page with names of those who signed the pledge. President Bill Clinton was impressed enough to hold a moving, nationally televised town forum in Akron to bring attention to the work. What the editor and publisher did was take a stand—a leadership role—on an issue that most of the community agreed was important. The question arose for many who shielded themselves behind the ethics code: Did our news organization cross a line? Can we take sides on an issue?

This, to me, was an important signal: newsrooms can, in fact, take the position that we want to participate with people in our community in efforts to improve life. The Pulitzer committee agreed. In 1994, *A Question of Color* won the Pulitzer gold medal for public service.

Drawing a Bigger Circle

At the People-Powered Publishing Conference in 2019, New York University journalism professor Jay Rosen offered that journalists gravitate to circles of power to do their work. Most people in power and journalists are college-educated, obsess about the news, have health care, eat well, and are paid above the median income level. In my own state, 70 percent of adults are not college graduates, and half make less than the median—both of which impact their ability to obtain other life essentials. Very few obsess about the news.

Saying it's time for media introspection feels a little like calling 9-1-1 for a house fire as the walls collapse inward. Innovators in People-Powered Publishing and Rosen, for years, have been warning that traditional journalism fails to honor citizens' desire to be knowledgeable and proactive participants in their communities.

I was feeling that desperation as assistant managing editor in the mid-1990s. I returned to reporting to experiment with people-driven public policy reporting, equipped with this newfound power of focus groups and a user-friendly Macintosh computer for the quantitative work.

The first project was on public education equity, a hot topic in polling. Ohioans identified quality education as critical to helping themselves and their children navigate a changing economy. Partnering with our statehouse bureau chief, Dennis Willard, we launched an exploration of public education based on site visits and original exploration of data. We discovered schools with 30-year-old textbooks, crumbling exterior walls with bricks tumbling onto the ground, some districts with several foreign languages and advanced placement classes while others had none, and communities incapable of financing an adequate education. But then, what is adequate? Willard and I had a gnawing question: How do we contrast the educational solutions enacted by politicians with Ohioans' thoughts on adequacy? The answer was found in a daylong dialogue designed by Rodgers and illustrated a vast gap between citizen expectations for public schools and what officials were addressing in the state capitol.

The tone of our coverage changed, causing our critics to accuse us of public school boosterism, or advocacy journalism. Our response was that our work was informed coverage. And anyone who suggested that our coverage was "advocacy journalism" on behalf of the public would cause us to respond that coverage of public policy from the perspective of government is advocacy on behalf of those in power.

The Rude Awakening

I returned to editing, oversaw projects on why people don't vote, the demise of the American Dream, surviving the Great Recession and a yearlong community civility project exploring polarization through a variety of lenses. I shared with Carolyn Lukensmeyer, then executive director of the National Institute for Civil Discourse, that there was a recurring theme in our dialogues: people blame media for the polarization. She selected Ohio as ripe for a deep dive on trust and polarization and designed a three-day retreat of citizens, leaders, and journalists. After a half day of cordialities, each group went to its respective private room and was asked to prepare a list of adjectives to describe each of the three groups on giant sheets of paper. Journalists were quick to describe leaders as corrupt, in it for power and money, and insensitive to the public's needs. For citizens, journalists listed "bored," "apathetic," and "not paying attention." Journalists said of themselves: "overworked, underappreciated professionals."

When the groups reconvened and posted their lists of descriptors for all to see, citizens were deeply hurt if not angered by the journalists. Their response was emotional. "You view us with disdain," one person said. By the end of the three days, journalists were shaken by the rebuke. The head of the Ohio Newspaper Association (now the Ohio News Media Association) was in the closing conversation with me, and we agreed to quickly convene interested news outlets to discuss and act on what we had learned. From that would grow the nation's largest statewide media collaborative, the Ohio Media Collaborative/Your Voice Ohio, which recognizes that newsrooms are a core problem in our democracy.

The newsroom executives who met in December 2015 in an outbuilding at the *Columbus Dispatch* printing plant weren't surprised when we described that embarrassing moment at Lukensmeyer's session. Newsrooms often had unhealthy attitudes toward complex communities. There was agreement that we needed to work together in the 2016 presidential election with these purposes: present the complexity of Ohio voices through robust public contact and polling, and do this collaboratively so that we produce and share an abundance of high-quality work.

A partnership with the Center for New Democratic Processes (CNDP), a nonprofit public research organization, and the Ray C. Bliss Institute of Applied Politics at the University of Akron, generated funding for a yearlong experiment of dialogue and polling along with shared reporting and editing that I managed out of the

Akron Beacon Journal. The CNDP hosted three three-day retreats in which citizens were asked to think about the role they wanted media to play.

Their responses could be boiled down to these suggestions:

- Give us charts and graphs that allow us to quickly gain an understanding of the issue at hand—our place in the community, state, nation, and time.

- Give us narratives of people who represent different life experiences and geographies and illustrate the complexity behind those charts and graphs. This allows us to weigh the ramifications of different solutions

- Otherwise, they said there was something missing from our reporting that enabled informed action on their part. We took that to mean solutions. In the case of the presidential election, we offered the platforms of Hillary Clinton and Donald Trump.

During the election campaign, media outlets took turns on the stories and jointly produced vignettes, charts, graphs, and photography. Each news package followed the suggestions above. In a final citizen jury designed by the CNDP, participants pointed to our work as different from other examples because ours gave them a feeling of being fully informed.

Yet, after this extraordinary reporting, many journalists still missed the full measure of the anger, resentment, and racism in Ohio after Hillary Clinton referred to many Trump supporters as a "basket of deplorables." Ohioans erected yard signs that said, "Deplorable and proud of it." Donald Trump won Ohio by eight points.

Collaboration, Solutions, and Engagement

While the national news media grappled in late 2016 with the question, "What the hell just happened?" Ohio journalists nonetheless were enthused about their collaborative experience. With funding acquired by the CNDP and dialogues designed by them, Ohio newsrooms were eager to continue collaboration and experimentation with an emphasis on media-sponsored community dialogue. From the initial dozen newsrooms working on the statewide election collaborative, Your Voice Ohio expanded over the next few years to build metro area collaboratives of competing outlets for the exploration of addiction, economic revival, racial equity, and quality of life. By the 2020 election, more than 50 news organizations representing legacy print and broadcast, alternative media, Black neighborhood monthlies, and online solutions-oriented outlets made up the nation's largest state media collaborative.

Just as people have different life experiences, so do journalists. After 46 years of continuous learning at the *Akron Beacon Journal*, I was able to segue in 2017 from managing Your Voice Ohio from my newsroom office to working with journalists and newsrooms all over the state (thanks to funding secured by CNDP). I met visionaries with traits that gave me hope: curiosity and respect for regular folks, commitment to service, and hunger for experimentation.

In the Youngstown-Warren area, media outlets are highly competitive and yet agreed to share resources and stories on one topic: the opioid crisis. Ohio repeatedly ranked in the top three states for overdose deaths per capita. Journalists had written stories ad nauseum yet the situation grew worse. The competing journalists gathered around a table at the Youngstown *Vindicator* (closed and sold a few years later) to discuss how the collaboration might work. A CNDP facilitator designed the two-hour conversations. We publicized them as sponsored by the news outlets and Your Voice Ohio. People felt safe to share intimate, heartbreaking experiences. Some who arrived expressing confidence that they had a solution soon realized that the problem was far more complex than they knew. Always, participants were asked to construct unique local solutions. After each session, journalists gathered to discuss what was learned. Journalists observed that people needed help more than they needed stories reminding them that there is an addiction crisis. Journalists also were taken by the disconnect between what was heard from community leaders and from people at the tables. In fact, journalists often noted that leaders who could have learned from the sessions weren't present.

In each session, participants included people struggling with addiction, families of victims, public officials, and the curious. I said, "There are journalists sitting at the tables *with you*. They're putting aside their competitive instincts to work together on this critical issue, to figure out how we can help." After the session in Warren, one of Ohio's most economically and drug-stressed cities, a woman raised her hand because she needed to say something: "Thank you so much for this. And you know what? I didn't know the news media cared."

"We didn't know the media cared" was a common refrain that jarred the journalists. Another common statement, this one from journalists, was: "I didn't know people could get along so well." Both of those realizations were transformative for reporters and editors.

All Journalism Is Advocacy Journalism

Advocacy, just like objectivity, needs a fresh definition. Former *New York Times* columnist Charlie Warzel rightly stated that newsworthiness is a choice masquerading as an inevitability. A newsroom decision to cover any government agency is a conscious decision that that agency is worthy of people's attention. Cover city council? All the time. Cover basic needs such as shelter, food, public transportation, and bodily functions? Not so much. Newsrooms cover criminal court but seldom wade into domestic relations court, even though local residents are far more likely to find themselves in divorce court. What are the reasons for that choice? (One court reporter told me divorce is "too messy.") The decision to cover any candidate for office suggests that that candidate is a viable option for voters. If that's not so, why do we argue about whether to include third-party candidates in media-sponsored debates? Likewise, choosing to cover the local task force on drug addiction gives voice to the professionals, or so-called experts. What voices are missing from that coverage? There are nearly 12 million people in Ohio. If we cover only the issues and solutions discussed by the few thousand elected officials—who already have dismissed issues they have no intention of fixing—we are advocates of officialdom in the public square. By choosing not to gain an understanding of the 12 million other Ohioans and represent them, we are saying to them that we are neither your representatives nor your advocates.

This is the reason I detest the phrase heard often when we're criticized for any particular story, "We're just holding up a mirror." By deciding where to point that mirror, we're advocating for one piece of news over another.

So, how do we decide which voices to amplify? Being *with people* in dialogue redefines our ideas of accountability, advocacy, and place. Being *with people* in conversation about problems and solutions makes us part of the community fabric as opposed to what Rosen calls "the view from nowhere."

Community dialogues on addiction that attracted multiple stakeholders in the Appalachian Parkersburg-Marietta area on the Ohio River illustrated most clearly how local media can inspire profound democratic action—and not solely with news stories. A group of local community organizers learned of the Your Voice Ohio initiative and offered to convene a meeting of local media and some mental health experts to see whether they would partner with us on opioids. The local organizers obtained funding for food and room rental and offered to handle publicity, meeting transcription, set-up, and tear-down. This was instructive for me because it illustrated the potential for partnerships that assisted the work of journalism without compromising journalists' work. We agreed to three events in three different communities and to a collaboration among six news outlets.

In the first session, several participants from a drug rehabilitation center arrived on a bus. Their compelling personal stories of decline into addiction and the strength they received from others in recovery stirred everyone. One elderly woman said she came with the idea that people just needed God, but afterward said she was overwhelmed by the complexity. A hospital representative who came with defensive messaging became an active listener. As for the people who came on the bus from the recovery center, they returned for the next session in the tiny hillside town of Belpre, and again for the third session in Marietta. Asked why they kept returning, one responded, "We finally feel like someone is listening."

For the final session in Marietta, about 35 people had preregistered. It was a hot night, and we met in a hard-to-find concrete block building at the fairgrounds. More than 80 showed up, among them a local judicial candidate, mental health workers, and several journalists; they all crowded into the aging, low-ceilinged room with its curled carpet and wobbly tables. The room was loud and there wasn't enough food, but ideas and stories flowed.

> The reporters who were unafraid to be seen as part of the community and engaged in good works were producing stories that resonated in daily life.

As the meeting closed with the listing of solutions, one of the men from the rehabilitation center said, "I'll tell you what we need. We need a hotline where you can get help when you need it." Almost in unison, community officials *and journalists* answered, "We do have a hotline," and several recited the number. His response: "Did *you* ever call the hotline number?" Of course not. Journalists and mental health professionals generally aren't in the depths of an opioid addiction and thus would have no reason to test the number. He explained that on a Saturday night, trying to decide between convulsive withdrawal and a potentially fatal overdose, he called the hotline, desperate for help. He was given a list of numbers to call on Monday during business hours to find someone who could schedule an appointment. That was not help in a crisis. The room grew very quiet as everyone processed a powerful moment—especially a few journalists who realized that maybe they had been guilty of parachute journalism *and* advocacy for officialdom.

Immediately after each session, I chatted with reporters about what they had learned. In Marietta, the noise in the building was too loud for us to talk, so we stepped into a grassy area outside. As we digested the meeting, I could see over reporters' shoulders as people spilled into the parking lot. They were hugging, exchanging phone numbers, writing notes. I had the reporters stop for a moment, turn around, and think about what they were seeing. More hugs. This outpouring of emotion was a result of journalists' willingness to work together on a community crisis. How did *we* feel about that? Their answers would come a week later, while sharing lunch around a long table. The reporters who were unafraid to be seen as part of the community and engaged in good works were producing stories that resonated in daily life.

This media-sponsored series had given a lot of people hope, and for good reason. A reporter later explored with the mental health service agency how the hotline could be reconfigured to be more helpful—and it was. A judicial candidate was elected and started a drug court. The community organizers, along with a local hospital and university, launched a study of the most effective forms of treatment, which changed treatment services in the valley. Journalism was the catalyst.

In more than 40 community sessions on a variety of topics, we learned that media-sponsored dialogue:

- empowers citizens to see shared values on which they can act independent of institutions.

- empowers responsible leaders with information about shared concerns and values in their community, and they are more willing to act accordingly.

- empowers journalists to rethink their vital role as participants with citizens in democratic processes and holding leaders accountable.

The End Times?

An unwillingness to experiment will be our demise. Likewise, a lack of understanding of how people in our communities have changed will be our demise. With my first story on the school board in 1971, and the newsroom coverage of the Goodyear takeover, I failed to recognize that the *Akron Beacon Journal's* market penetration was so deep—at times we had the highest household penetration in the country—that any gathering of people eventually turned to the news. Today, with so few people accessing traditional local news sites, those news outlets are no longer the primary catalyst for dialogue and action. We aren't part of the living fabric.

One has to wonder whether Jim Batten saw this diminution in value coming 30 years ago. His enthusiasm for engagement, perhaps, was misinterpreted by some journalists as a means of convincing people we have something of value when, in fact, what he meant was that engagement is a tool for knowing how and what news is of value to people.

And what is of value? A photographer once argued at an Ohio journalism event that photos of courtroom drama draw eyeballs. Their online analytics prove it. My questions: How important was that drama to narratives that serve the community, and what are the demographics of people who are clicking on those photos? If we have pruned our online audience of readers who crave complexity and problem-solving because we have too little of it, are those photo clicks then coming from a crowd seeking entertainment? At many news outlets, including ours, we went beyond the number of times people clicked on a story to include the amount of time they actually spent on the story, known as time on site. Outstanding enterprise work, which did poorly in the daily click count, rose to the top when analyzed for time on site over the next several weeks.

This brings us full circle. Is journalism indeed a catalyst? Scientifically, the term refers to an element that remains unaltered as it enables other elements to be transformed. Maybe that's the problem: we are indeed catalysts, unchanging over the decades. The democratic actions we once provoked are now provoked more effectively by others. Thus, people continue to engage in dialogue and to participate in democratic practices, though sometimes poorly—or even destructively—informed, but without us.

Where does that leave journalism? What should we do, or be?

We should be integral, vital, living threads in the fabric of democracy, stretching and flexing so that people see us as partners, as vital to improving their lives. That means we must pick sides. We have to favor improvement in living conditions, opportunities to achieve dreams, democratic participation, and facilitate all of those in new ways.

That means we should never again hear someone say, "I didn't know the media cared."

Fostering Human Connection Is the Heart of Media Reform

by Michelle Holmes

Perhaps the simplest way to measure a healthy democracy is whether its people use "we/ours" or "they/theirs" when they speak of public life.

Our schools.
Our prisons.
Our parks.
Our vaccination rates.
Our maternal health indicators.
Our taxation rates.
Our representatives in Washington, DC.

When connected by common purpose, "We the People" come together to govern ourselves.

That sense of "us" must come from someplace, of course, and for much of the history of the United States of America, that place was newspapers.

Indeed, for generations, American newspapers and American democracy appeared to coexist in a winding double helix: as Americans we knew ourselves primarily through the stories we read in our newspapers, then later via radio and TV broadcasts.

From small towns to big cities, each day's edition reflected a community's image back to itself through front pages, crime pages, sports pages, and society pages, allowing its readers to form a view of themselves in relation to the whole.

Newspapers served as the primary forum for the important questions:

Who shall govern us and how?
What is the plan for economic growth and change?
How do we treat our poorest citizens?
How do we educate our children?

And as compiler of the quotidian:

Our sports scores.
Our house break-ins.
Our school lunch menus.
Our engagements and our deaths.

Each edition was a fabric of many lives. Delivered to your doorstep. The story of "us."

Despite this role in a democratic system, the vast majority didn't "get the paper" out of a patriotic duty; it was simply the best way to circulate information that was available, advertise goods and services, and save that which was notable or useful. It was a product of commerce that supported an intrinsic human need: connection with the whole.

While much has been made of the political accountability, civic information, and education that news media has offered in its role as the Fourth Estate, this essay seeks to share the view that a vital and mostly unrecognized legacy of the journalism industry—as well as its future promise—is its creation of a locus of belonging to a place and its people.

It means the local news media's greatest impact is to be understood as something greater than tellers of tales, compilers of facts, or uncoverers of injustice, but also as mirrors that have allowed humans to see themselves in relation to the whole, and to feel their own place inside of it.

Traditional hard news was part of that, but so was a community calendar, letters to the editor, "athlete of the week," gardening columnists who told you when the peonies would bloom, photos of grandfathers in the park fishing with children, and many other kinds of stories, explorations, conversations, and gatherings that happened around a central core that helped us know our fellow citizens. Who played varsity basketball? Who ran the local department store? Who were the rebels and the changemakers and the artists? It wasn't just telling stories. Newspapers also sponsored community banquets, food drives, and events that actively contributed to a secular civic square.

This is not centered in nostalgia. Rather, it's looking back beyond the journalism itself to the multifaceted role that news organizations played at the center of civic life for much of the history of our nation.

"We (Some of) the People"

Of course, like the birth of American democracy itself, the news industry model was deeply and tragically flawed in its inherent state of exclusion, the mirror it held up reflected a world in which some people were deemed less worthy and less equal than the others.

Just as our nation's Founding Fathers enshrined the notion of freedom to "the People" and meant only White men, the local newspaper (or local TV newscast) established a certain brand of "us" as defined by the dominant, overwhelmingly White, male cultural narrative of the day, marked by catchphrases such as the *New York Times*'s "All the news that's fit to print" and Walter Cronkite's "And that's the way it is."

As this publishes some two years after the radical racial awakening of post-George Floyd America (which followed the Me Too movement's reckoning with the abuses of women in public and private workplaces everywhere), it's easier for more people to see that systemic racism and patriarchal, heteronormative standards shaped the very core of what was news because the mainstream newspaper was a product of (and tool of) that broader racist, sexist mainstream thought.

Perhaps it seems naive to believe a battered (and often battering) modern news media can reinvent itself as a democratic tool to connect all Americans.

In practice, that meant the news media's pages and practices long reflected the mores of the day simply as "the way things were" in subtle, systemic, and overt ways, even as many news organizations pursued important reporting that challenged the harm created by those mores and the policies they were historically (and often concurrently) part of creating.

From the vantage point of 2023, decades of disruptions in the old, hierarchical media model—in which an editor decides the "most important" news of the day, while an editorial board tells a community what to think and how to act—feel like a necessary correction.

What comes to replace it, of course, is a work in progress, with many committed doers and thinkers in journalism seeking new ways for our human collective to gather, join together, and tell our stories.

Many of the essays in this volume point at alternative ways of thinking about an evolving journalism as a partner of evolving democracy, extending journalism's legacy as a shaper of collective meaning through a new and modern mirror capable of reflecting all of us as equal, free, and worthy.

Perhaps it seems naive to believe a battered (and often battering) modern news media can reinvent itself as a democratic tool to connect all Americans—no matter our skin tone, gender, sexual orientation, and abilities—to an embodied sense of "We the People" who have agreed to live under common, elected governance freely chosen from our own ranks, sharing duties and responsibilities for the common good, and seeing others as inherently worthy as ourselves.

Yet the bones of this news-industry-as-collective-meaning-maker of our times and the important legal press protections that have been carved out over two centuries as a tool for the free exchange of ideas have the capacity to serve as a foundation upon which to begin to tell a new, common story of our humanity in the 21st century and to bring us together—literally—in new ways.

Experiments in a More Connected Journalism

Journalism is not a practice that can be done conceptually. Any ideas of what "should work" quickly meet the rubber of the marketplace road. My sudden first-person entry into this essay here (hello there!) is for the purposes of contextualizing and situating the concepts I'm discussing in a real American newsroom.

In 2012, Advance Local, a national newspaper company, embarked on a serious digital strategy and hired me to take them forward into unknown territory. I arrived in 2013 in Birmingham, Alabama, as vice president of content and later, leaving the newsroom, began overseeing expansion and development work in digital media and TV and film development.

My colleagues and coconspirators from 2013 to 2019 were committed and talented local journalists with generational roots in Alabama, along with a cadre of local and visiting thinkers, visionaries, filmmakers, and practitioners of storytelling as a democratic practice who came to experiment, learn, and contribute in Alabama.

As I reflect over hundreds of initiatives small and large aimed at creating a more democratic press, three foundational principles come to mind. I share these here, along with examples from Alabama, as the undergirding of the work as I came to understand it. I encourage you, reader, to see what you would add or subtract from this list as you read the other essays of this same volume.

1. A recognition by news organizations that helping citizens understand ourselves as part of the whole—I see you and you see me *and we are all in this together*—is among their core contributions to democracy.

2. Actively creating environments—via storytelling, staffing, and vision—inclusive of a broader "us" that more fully reflect the rich diversity of the 21st century.

3. Creating spaces online and in person where people can directly connect with one another in healthy and productive ways that encourage a healthy democracy.

The examples I share below from 2013 to 2019—*Whitman, Alabama,* It's a Southern Thing, and Reckon South—are taken from hundreds of experimental efforts, small and large, by Alabama Media Group journalists and collaborators. Each principle is highlighted in these examples and shows specific ways in which connecting people can be part of the product itself.

Whitman, Alabama

Principle No. 1: A recognition by news organizations that helping citizens understand ourselves as part of the whole—I see you and you see me *and we are all in this together*—is among their core contributions to democracy.

In her sprawling experimental documentary project *Whitman, Alabama*, journalist and filmmaker Jennifer Crandall set out to connect herself to the people of Alabama and to connect the people of Alabama to one another and to the world.

Crandall conceived of and created the Whitman project—Alabamians reciting Walt Whitman's 19th century poem "Song of Myself" on video—while she was an artist-in-residence at Alabama Media Group, a post created to stretch the bounds of the journalistic form. The project has since been studied by scholars at Cambridge University, screened at festivals in Macau and Rome, and installed in major exhibitions in New York and Philadelphia.

"Ultimately the idea of the project is to get people to recognize that we need to understand and to know each other better," Crandall said in an interview with the National Endowment for the Arts. "I want to show the richness of people. I want to create work that somehow sparks in a viewer a connection. I think what Walt Whitman does is he makes us large when he says, 'I contain multitudes.' . . . If you can recognize the largeness within yourself, then you should recognize that within other people."

As a piece of American art that focuses its lens on the inherent light of the human condition, the videos are a reminder that a news organization's most ambitious work does not have to center always on corruption or wrongdoing but can help share the beauty and inherent worth and dignity of the very human beings a news organization serves.

Alabama Media Group's multiyear funding for the work—which was later also supported by the Ford Foundation—showed a commitment to using the resources of the news organization to explore new ways of seeing and knowing one another as we attempt to live together.

The hundreds of deeply personal letters we received in response to this project spoke to a deep and moving recognition of belonging to something bigger that the project engendered in its viewers.

I lived in Alabama 45 years, writing poetry, supporting the arts with a little organization for artists. I did this working two jobs and being a single mom. I live in NYC these days; I am 48 years old. I am the American writer for Jazz in Europe. *I have a son your age, he lives in Chattanooga and is a working artist. You would think that I would have a sense of myself, but I don't. Always searching, always seeking, always reaching. Your documentary gave a very precious part of myself back to me. It is a beautiful and remarkable project and I thank you from all the bottom of my Alabama heart.*

Becca

I have to thank you personally for creating your beautiful project. It is a touch of perfection and in this climate, it fills me with a touch of hope. Can I say that it brings me to fresh tears each time and I am not sure why? Perhaps my heart hears a forgotten tongue and is answering in recognition. And can I tell you, it makes me fall in love with this country even more? I am nothing like the people I see here. I am just like people I see here. With this verse and their voice, you are crafting a perfect strand of pearls.

Be well,
Georgia

Your film is a miracle. The dignity, the humanity of these people is just . . . the dignity, the humanity of the language. . . . I am writing this through tears.

"Thank you" doesn't come near.
Adam

Your project is one of the greatest examples of art's power to showcase the commonalities in American society that are most often dismissed, or denied, in favor of our dwelling on our differences. . . . Thank you for reminding all Americans of the greatness we are capable of when we look at one another as equals.

Henry

This work now continues as an independent project headed by Crandall. It can be seen at https://whitmanalabama.com/.

It's a Southern Thing

Principle No. 2: Actively creating environments—via storytelling, staffing, and vision—inclusive of a broader "us" that more fully reflect the rich diversity of the 21st century.

It's a Southern Thing is the name of a viral comedy brand run by Alabama Media Group's Red Clay Media division. It was developed by listening to southerners hungry for someone to see them and "get them," beyond the ugly stereotypes. That listening happened in many ways, led by careful insight into audience analytics that helped its leadership team, Elizabeth Hoekenga and Justin Yurkanin, understand the giant appetite for content that spoke to the southern experience in ways that were not preachy, judgmental, or dismissive. Eventually, a reader ecosystem formed that allowed the brand's audience to serve as co-creators as they shared a constant stream of southern phrases, ideas, and shared experiences around food and family and place, with a goal to welcome people to gather together.

It's a Southern Thing describes itself like this:

> We celebrate the things that unite Southerners. Sometimes we laugh at ourselves—but we're allowed to do that. After all, we're Southern, too. . . . Southerners often see themselves misrepresented in popular culture, and our goal is to change that. . . . A Facebook fan once commented that we're "the friendliest corner of the internet" and we aim to create that kind of experience for our audience every day.[1]

Certainly, this brand, built around jokes about cornbread and sweet tea will never be a satisfying place for those expecting to do the work of radical social reform. But for those who see it as I do—as a reflection of a new and healthier "center" in a polarized world and a new, more inclusive perception of southern values—it offers hope in its gentle and inclusive humor. Beyond videos and articles, It's a Southern Thing continues to create new ways to bring its fans together live online in game shows, contests, virtual gaming, and other spaces of friendly connection, fueled by the powerful medicine of shared laughter.

As a media brand born from a newsroom's roots, it has sought to create a respectful and polite place to celebrate being together with millions of others across political and social lines in an increasingly polarized age.

This is not to say this brand's audience of more than 5 million followers has somehow morphed into a utopian community, nor is it to say the brand has fully achieved its "commitment to making It's a Southern Thing an inclusive, antiracist community." Yet, It's a Southern Thing continues its work actively and overtly creating an updated story of "us" in the mainstream South. That work is building trust in the public interest—so much, in fact, that Birmingham's public radio station WBHM turned to this comedy brand to produce a highly viewed series of short TikTok videos (funded by a grant from the Corporation for Public Broadcasting) to address vaccine misinformation among 18- to 30-year-olds in the South, demonstrating the trust it has gained among its audience.

While this is a new kind of online fellowship around positive shared values, it is also a commercial endeavor, attracting new forms of advertising collaboration that values a wildly engaged community of fans.

The following exchange of just 6 of 2,400 comments on one comedic video called *Moms Can Solve ANY Problem* offers some insight into the kinds of conversations people develop in a place that's curated for connection:[2]

> *I wish I could call my mama. HA she's too selfish and doesn't care to help me. But if any of y'all have great moms then lucky you.—A. M. S.*
>
> *A. M. S., how sad for you and sorry.—B. A.*
>
> *B. A., ya it is what it is I guess. It's pretty hurtful for sure. It seems some individuals in this world are forgetting to see what's really important.—A. M. S.*
>
> *A. M. S., I am sorry. Hopefully you can find an older lady in your neighborhood or work to fill that void. And maybe someday she will realize how valuable you are to her. ♥ —K. A. M.*
>
> *K. A. M., Thank you for your kind words. I hope so too but I doubt she'll see. 🙏♥—A. M. S.*

More of It's a Southern Thing's interactive fan community can be experienced on Facebook at https://www.facebook.com/itisasouthernthing/.

Reckon South and Reckon Women

Principle No. 3: Creating spaces online and in person where people can directly connect with one another in healthy and productive ways that encourage a healthy democracy.

In May 2019, when Alabama passed the nation's most restrictive abortion law, Alabama Media Group's current vice president of content, Kelly Ann Scott, and her team solicited and received hundreds of essays from women with views across the political and social spectrum and published them as the sole content of the news sections in the *Birmingham News*, the *Huntsville Times,* and the Mobile *Press-Register.* Suddenly, women's voices *were* the news because a woman editor in charge decided they were. In fact, they were deemed all of the news that was fit to print in the newspaper's first section that day, in a first-of-its kind, historic American newspaper.

The team followed immediately with the creation of Reckon Women, a Facebook group dedicated to discussing the issues of Alabama women, under the social media-focused Reckon South brand.[3]

> Suddenly, women's voices *were* the news because a woman editor in charge decided they were.

More than 1,000 women joined within the first 24 hours. The team partnered with Spaceship Media to guide the group's members through two years of in-depth discussions and connections. This gathering of women across the political spectrum led to an in-person connection at the state's capital where women gathered to learn about how they could become involved in the state's political process.

Learnings from the Reckon Women group led to experimental new approaches to intersectional coverage and connection that continue into 2023 under the Reckon South umbrella—including *Black Joy,*[4] a newsletter focusing on joy as a path to Black liberation, and *Honey,*[5] a newsletter community designed to serve young women and LGBTQ+ readers, which the brand calls the "girls, gays and theys" of the South—as well as new partnerships to convene "community-building" conversation among younger audiences.

We see you, this journalism seems to say, and we are glad you are here.

These examples offer insight into ways just one news organization has worked to offer new kinds of experiences for people to come together to play a part in their communities.

I do not ask myself, or you, to presume that these are perfect, or enough. As we trace journalism's role in the 21st century, however, they serve as interesting places of study and consideration, and perhaps as inspiration for new experiments and ideas to flourish.

The time has never been riper for journalism to come to the aid of democracy.

Democracy's Threat

It's likely we are living in the loneliest time in human history.

Through millions of years, as we developed as a species, we relied on the daily physical presence of other humans for our very survival.

Now for the first time in our planet's history, it's possible for large portions of the population to simply stay inside, alone, in a new kind of Door-Dashing, Peloton-riding, Netflix-watching, telehealthing, virtual-schooling, Fortnite-gaming, online-church-going modern life.

Even before the pandemic, people's experience of loneliness had been rising for most of the last century, driven by myriad social changes. Urbanization trends have brought us together physically closer than ever before, while creating conditions in which fewer people know their neighbors; the rise of the handheld smartphone has brought a new paradoxical entry into the human condition in the form of the ubiquitous screen that both connects and isolates us.

The statistics are staggering.

The percentage of Americans who say they have no close friends has quadrupled since 1990, according to the Survey Center on American Life. Fifty-four percent of Americans report sometimes or always feeling that no one knows them well, according to a 2018 Ipsos survey. A 2020 Harvard study suggests that 36 percent of all Americans—including 61 percent of young adults and 51 percent of mothers with young children—feel "serious loneliness."

The heightened risk of mortality from loneliness equals that of smoking 15 cigarettes a day or being an alcoholic and exceeds the health risks associated with obesity, according to research by Julianne Holt-Lunstad, professor of psychology and neuroscience at Brigham Young University.

Feelings of loneliness are not the culprit, experts say.[6] Just as hunger pangs signal a need for the body to eat to keep it healthy, the sadness, agitation, and depression of loneliness are signals for a human to seek out the kind of healthy relationships that will ensure better psychobiological health.

The challenge in loneliness, many studies show, is that when those relationships aren't (or can't be) developed, a host of mental and physical conditions, including low self-esteem, depression, irritability, and suspicion of others, make it *harder* to connect with others, spiraling lonely people into even greater states of despair and disconnection.[7]

It's not just individual or collective happiness, however, that is at stake.

Those who study the rise of political extremism have long warned that the crippling effects of social isolation are showing up in the radicalization of lonely people around the world.

Political philosopher Hannah Arendt sounded this alarm in 1951 when she published *The Origins of Totalitarianism,* in which she wrote, "Totalitarian domination . . . bases itself on loneliness, on the experience of not belonging to the world at all, which is among the most radical and desperate experiences of man."[8]

As democracies around the globe begin to buckle under the weight of people unable to come together to see common ground to govern themselves peacefully, it's clear that new social structures must arise.

And while technology may have played a role at disconnecting us from one another, the advances of technology married with human wisdom and empathy can support humans in creating and maintaining the kind of social structures that allow us to feel our lives matter— that we are seen, heard, felt, and known by other human beings in ways that help us feel meaning and value in our lives.

A Body Politic with Room for All Bodies

Today, to play a role in a democracy, one has the right to vote, to run for office, and to lobby elected officials.

And what if there was something more? What if you had a *right* to a place in the body politic?

A world in which billions of people have access to online "Citizen Circles" as part of the fundamental human process of self-governance and self-care in an increasingly isolated age could ensure that *all* people—including the disabled and homebound—have a place to be heard, seen, and felt by other people as a core human right.

Indeed, the United Nations' Universal Declaration of Human Rights offers us the raw material for such an idea when it declares we, the people of the earth, hold "the right to . . . equal access to public service in one's country" and "the right to participate in the cultural life of the community."[9]

So far as I know, this vision of a world where there is a place for everyone lives now only in my dreamtime.

Despite a global pandemic, no replicable, large-scale public models have emerged that exist to bring humans into real-time connection for the purpose of mitigating the deleterious personal and societal effects of loneliness and social isolation by connecting one another's stories and experiences to serve the common good.

Yet I share this dream, to close this essay, in answer to the question, "What role might journalism play in strengthening democracy?" as an outgrowth of my time and thinking as a journalist and as a human.

Already, the pull to connect is big business. Hundreds of billions of dollars are being poured into the creation of a metaverse and other virtual, immersive worlds with the express aim of helping people feel more connected in online spaces. As new and socially attractive forms of public connection are created, new chances to monetize this human need will arrive as well.

To function well, such citizen connection spaces and practices should feel like welcoming, fun, and enjoyable leisure activities that feel good, offer value, support happier lives, and be created by people who understand how to build real connection among communities.

Luckily, news organizations don't have to wait for "someday" to experiment right now with all kinds of connecting as part of their core mission: calling their own dreams, ideas, and innovations online and in person; strengthening their commitment to the communities they serve; and inviting new opportunities for community collaboration to ensure old discriminatory and exclusionary practices of the past are left behind.

In fact, news organizations have a chance to recommit to a historic mission when they understand that healthy human connection—the very antidote to loneliness—is, and always has been, at the very center of their existence as shapers of communities and convenors of the civic square.

"We the People" are waiting for the invitation to arrive.

Moving Forward, Joined Together

Creating a culture that supports new democratic practices will require a radical rethinking of the work of journalism.

As I have transitioned from practicing journalism to supporting the work of leaders and dreamers, I've been deeply fortunate to join forces with listening poet and racial healer Salaam Green and mental health reformer and psychologist Lucy Wairimu Mukuria to hold space for people in deep inquiry into personal and collective change.

As the forces of human freedom are waging a battle with old patriarchal forces through acceptance of LGBTQ+ rights and women's rights, and a reckoning with structural racism's past and present, human consciousness is moving forward with all the angst that entails. New structures will necessarily spring up to support new human expression.

Often, this cultural upheaval we citizens of the world in 2023 are part of together can seem harsh and unrelenting, offering no place to pause and rest and take stock of our progress in building a world where all our voices can be heard.

Often there's no place to dream the world we want into being.

So, to close this essay, I invite you into such a moment now.

I invite you, journalists and non-journalists alike, skeptics and cynics, those who pray, and those who hope, to take a moment to listen to what democracy feels like inside of you and allow it to inspire your own dreams and actions.

This is mine. I would love to hear yours.

> A Democracy Heart-Song
> Our beloved country,
> Our beloved world,
> Our beloved us,
> Our tired and frightened and brave and angry and
> beautiful people,
> Bring us strength to be free together.

None of Us Do This Alone

The examples in this essay represent just a sampling of the new approaches one media organization has been exploring. They are evidence of a move afoot to use the tools of a free press in the service of a free people. For this kind of change to take root, it requires a national community of journalists engaged in creating new practices, including my fellow authors of this volume, each of whom has inspired and encouraged me.

I am especially grateful to Alabama Media Group president Tom Bates and the ownership of Advance Local, and to K. A. Turner and Bob Sims because I would have been literally cast out of Alabama without them. I am also grateful to Spaceship Media, JSK Fellowships, Hearken, Tiny Collaborative, Journalism That Matters, Center for Investigative Reporting, the Kettering Foundation, and to the David Mathews Center for Civic Life, among several other organizations and friends, for the important creative and emotional support of our work during my time in Alabama. My thanks also to Paula Ellis and Paloma Dallas for creating a gracious, warm space for me to feel heard; to David Mathews for his lifelong honoring of the role of citizen; to my husband and journalist Murdoch Davis, an intellectual and heart partner in seeing journalism's future; and to Spaceship Media cofounder Eve Pearlman for her broad vision and contributions to many of my unfolding ideas.

Dream Forward Together

I invite you to try an exercise in imagining. It can be carried out as a private contemplation or through journaling or it can become fodder for a conversation with friends over cocktails. You can do it whether you are a reporter, newsroom leader, minister, firefighter, or a human of no particular occupation who hopes for a brighter future.

Imagine yourself sitting in a park in your community. Pick a comfortable bench where you can relax for the next 20 minutes. Feel the sunshine on your face. Now imagine that a person, *very unlike you* in race, gender, income, sexual orientation, ethnicity, religion, and hobbies, is sitting on a bench directly across from you. Build a clear picture of that person and make sure you know his, her, or their name. Ask this person if you can climb inside their head for a little while. Imagine they say yes. Imagine you can let go of judgment, just for today.

Now, for 10 minutes, I invite you to do your best to see life the way they actually see it and answer the following questions either by writing or sharing with others out loud:

What does that person need to feel safe?

What does that person dream of?

What is the first thing they think of when they wake up in the morning?

What is the last thing they think of when they are falling asleep?

What does that person need to feel a part of "your" community?

Again, really get a sense of being inside this person and do your best to answer. (Note: you can consider—but are not limited to—the questions of this exercise.)

If you were going to build a local news organization to serve the actual needs of this person as stated in the exercise, for what reason and how often would that person choose to engage with it?

Imagine this person valued this organization enough to pay $20 per month for it. In their words, what are they paying for?

Is there anything you would need to change or add to make it valuable for you, too?

If that organization were successful in delivering value to this person, what are three big or small ways the life of this person might change?

If that organization were successful in delivering value to both of you ("our" news organization, you might call it), how might your community change?

Thank your imaginary partner! Let them know your three big takeaways from being inside their head. Exchange phone numbers. Keep talking.

If you enjoyed this imaginary exercise, repeat with an actual person (or two), and see how results vary.

Dismantling Systemic Racism in News

by Martin G. Reynolds

It feels difficult at this moment to return to the summer of George Floyd's killing.

I remember sitting in my car, rewatching the video on my phone, listening to accounts of protests. Hearing about Breonna Taylor and the list of other Black men and women and people of color killed by police was overwhelming.

I was enraged.
I was distraught.
I was scared.
I was ready to fight back.
How best to do that?

I decided I would never allow a police officer to press the life out of me. Trust in following police commands had been broken in a way I hadn't before experienced.

There was something about that time that felt profoundly different from other instances of police violence that I had helped cover or witnessed during my journalism career.

This time, tears of rage streamed down my face as I sat in my car.

Something snapped me out of a state of the journalistic objectivity that had guided my view of these stories and tragedies throughout my years as a journalist. This felt different and I could no longer separate my own Blackness and humanity from Floyd and from Taylor, slain in her own apartment by police following a no-knock warrant that was not issued for her.

For those reading this who aren't journalists and who must be bewildered at how such separation from tragedy can be navigated, I must explain that I, among so many of my colleagues, was schooled in the objective approach to journalism.

I was taught that you kept your views on these issues from entering the coverage of a story, agreeing to a certain kind of internal invisibility. You are the witness, not the participant. You are the storyteller, not a character in the story.

I was instructed that who you are and what you have experienced have no place in the framing of a piece. You articulate what happened, with context of course. But often straight news stories about an incident weren't the place for nuance and deep historical context. In the world of daily newspaper journalism where I was forging a career, you had to keep it moving. "You can always do a *folo* (the journalistic term for a next-day story)," one of my former editors would say as she pounded out succinct edits on deadline.

News always happened the next day, so you moved on to the next homicide, fire, robbery, or carjacking. Or, perhaps the bit of context you did insert was removed or challenged by an editor or cut by the copy desk for space or because an editor thought it wasn't appropriate.

I realize now that the invisibility extended beyond the role of journalist to a deeper place. I had to embrace the invisibility to survive, to find my place, to belong. But it wasn't a true belonging.

I was taught that you kept your views on these issues from entering the coverage of a story, agreeing to a certain kind of internal invisibility.

Early in my career, I felt I had to compress elements of my identity and learn to turn away from the experiences that shaped my perception of the world. It wasn't something that anyone necessarily said. It was more subtle and yet profound.

As that summer of violence and protest was unfolding, my initial instinct was to maintain my objectivity and to frame my view of these horrible events through the lens of a media professional and not a Black man with his own Black son.

Countless cases of Black and Brown people slain by police over the years hadn't shaken that training, even though I felt pain each time it happened. The blatant racism on the part of police was something I had experienced many times, particularly as a young man, and I always felt as though it eroded my belief in democratic institutions. The conflict of being a taxpayer and feeling under threat is a paradox I was never surprised by.

As I reflect on this, now that some time has passed since the summer of Floyd and Taylor (which was followed by an insurrection fomented by a sitting president), I will say that my faith in democratic institutions does not have the luxury of being eroded by individuals not worthy of serving in them.

Looking at how representatives in the Trump administration, Congress, and even the spouse of a Supreme Court justice have behaved and perpetuated lies they know to be untrue has in some strange way evolved my view of the importance of these flawed but vital institutions.

Either the institutions themselves must be dismantled and rebuilt from the ground up or individuals with honor and integrity must stand up and lean against the pillars of these institutions and offer support to their cracking foundations.

I must admit that I am not sure which of these makes the most sense, or if either makes any sense.

As a member of one of these institutions—the Fourth Estate, as the news media is often referred to—I have an obligation to protect the parts of my institution that are honorable, that do great work, and that endeavor to expose harm and hold power accountable. And if there are outlets and individuals who won't do the hard work to fix and address the harm they do, then their legacies should not guarantee their survival.

And as news outlets scrambled to cover Floyd's killing, something clearly snapped within them. The people who had so often been invisible were demanding to be seen.

The reckoning in the streets, where we heard calls for racial justice, were echoed in newsrooms.

And there is a damn good reason for that.

Fairly recently, newspapers, including the *Orlando Sentinel*, *Los Angeles Times*, *Kansas City Star*, *Baltimore Sun*, and the *Philadelphia Inquirer*, have, in various ways, admitted and apologized for their histories of racist coverage and the inflaming of racial tensions.

In a compelling Poynter Institute series, Mark I. Pinsky, author and former staff writer for the *Orlando Sentinel* wrote:

> In recent years, a handful of the region's newspapers have stepped forward to accept responsibility for biased reporting and editorials, shouldering their share of the burden of racist Southern history. They are acknowledging—belatedly—what their forebearers did and did not do in covering racism, White supremacy, terror and segregation over the past 150 years. Some newspapers, including the *Sentinel*, had especially grievous sins to confess.[1]

The *Inquirer*'s look into its history, which was done by Pulitzer Prize-winning journalist Wesley Lowery, also apologized for the harm it had caused to Black journalists who worked for the paper, in addition to the Black community.

"The journalistic examination of the *Inquirer* by Wesley Lowery published this week [February 2022] puts our failings in brutal relief," wrote Elizabeth H. Hughes, the paper's publisher. "The reporting shows not only that we have not done right—it reveals, starkly, that we have done wrong. Black voices in the story—inside and outside the newsroom—articulate forcefully the harm we have inflicted over decades."[2]

So often, mainstream news organizations acted as though they were above the failings of these other institutions, as though the journalism we were practicing was somehow the linchpin to a more honorable place in the morass of a messy democracy. When, in fact, these news organizations were no better, inflicted harm, and perpetuated systemic racism and White supremacy just as the police and courts have done.

These pillars of democracy were reflections of what was happening outside newsrooms. And in a way, perhaps they were even worse because so many in them perceived themselves to be different and they weren't. Shame on them for thinking they ever were.

The questions for me remain, What will be the true impact of these apologies? What will change, especially given the ongoing challenges around revenue, the perpetual lack of diversity in these institutions, and the fact that many White people in them have not reckoned with their own internalized White supremacy?

You can't change an institution if the majority of the people inside it are unable, unwilling, or don't know how, to unwind decades of socialized racism and bias.

It is that racism and bias that have left so many feeling invisible, like they don't belong in the very profession they have worked so hard to join.

I have to admit I never expected to "belong" in my newsroom.

I was taught to endure, by journalists of color who were older and wiser. There wasn't anything close to the refreshing expectation of "cultural competence" on the part of the institution that some younger millennials and Gen Zs have now come to call for.

I am glad they are, but that was not the reality I stepped into. The preparation I received was in the form of encouragement to sustain; to expect the arrows, the lack of cultural humility, blatant ignorance, and tone deafness; and to push through it in service of my career and the need for more journalists of color in the newsroom.

We were prepared by journalists of color who were boomers and who were shaped by the experiences of their times and who were steeped in the civil rights movement. I was taught to understand that, in many ways, my presence was a form of protest.

> You can't change an institution if the majority of the people inside it are unable, unwilling, or don't know how, to unwind decades of socialized racism and bias.

My career began as a Chips Quinn Scholar intern at the *Oakland (CA) Tribune* in 1995. The program was started by former Gannett newspaperman John Quinn and his wife Lowy to build diversity across newsrooms. It was named after their son, John "Chips" Quinn Jr., who was a newspaper editor in upstate New York when he died in an automobile accident.

I grew up in Berkeley, just next door to Oakland, and knew "The Town," as it is affectionately called. I went to Merritt and Laney community colleges, both in Oakland, and lived in West Oakland at the time of the 1989 Loma Prieta earthquake that snapped part of the

Bay Bridge and pancaked the Cypress Freeway, which ran parallel to my neighborhood. That earthquake, and the experience covering parts of the aftermath, cemented my pursuit of journalism. At the time, I was writing for Merritt's paper and produced a first-person piece about being at ground zero of some of the worst damage the quake had caused.

I don't recall exactly how the opportunity came to pass. All I know is that Erna Smith (a former San Francisco State University journalism department professor who later became chair) and Charles Jackson (a longtime journalist and later editor of the *Tribune*) were key figures in my landing the internship that launched my career. Both were Black folks who were pioneers, and as Smith used to quip, "It's exhausting being in the vanguard."

The still-on-his-beat-to-this-day *Tribune* cop reporter Harry Harris sent me out to one of my first stories. It was to the home of a family whose loved one had been shot and killed in East Oakland. It is hard to describe the feeling of going up to the front door of a parent who has lost a child to violence. "I am sorry for disturbing you. Would you like to tell me something about your son?" Looking back, I realize just how invasive it must have been. I was compassionate, but I did not possess the understanding of a kind of slowness that such a responsibility requires.

I was just trying not to screw up. I didn't want to hurt the family any further, fail my editor, or miss an opportunity to beat the competition. I didn't grasp the gravity of what I was doing or the magnitude of what I was asking for. I was asking for a trust I had not yet earned.

I embraced my training and schooling, which taught me that I was there to try and tell the story, to offer a cathartic opportunity for loved ones to share on what was likely the worst day of their life.

I realize now that there is an affliction infecting journalism, and this affliction is haste. The very thing that we pride ourselves on is the very thing that often causes harm. One of the core tenets of daily journalism is urgency.

Author and activist Tema Okun, in an essay written about White supremacy culture, cites "sense of urgency" as among its core traits—a "continued sense of urgency that makes it difficult to take time to be inclusive, encourage democratic and/or thoughtful decision-making, to think long-term, to consider consequences.[3]

The alignment with daily journalism is chilling, and this has only deepened as social media platforms and a news culture of "post early and often" has trained news consumers to have a voracious appetite for information, often fed at the expense of care and intentionality.

When I was at the *Tribune*, I wrote about so many people who were killed in Oakland. I endeavored to remain "objective" because that was what I was taught to do in journalism school.

I know now that teaching objectivity to journalists is like teaching vegetarianism to a lion.

There certainly are objective facts, but even objective facts are seen through the lens of who we are and how we show up as human beings. It's why two people can look at the same events or an issue and come away with very different perceptions about what happened or what is at stake.

Objective facts can tell only part of the story, leaving out the nuance of how an issue affects people across the social fault lines and intersections of race, class, gender, generation, geography, sexual orientation, politics, religion, or level of ability.

I was struck by the wisdom of Gabriel Kahn, a professor of professional practice at the University of Southern California Annenberg School for Communication and Journalism, who talked about objectivity as an invention on the part of mainstream news outlets to grow revenue and audience. There wasn't some altruistic reason for it, as Kahn explained during a session of his that I attended as part of a Maynard Institute program. It was about not pissing people off so news outlets could attract more readers, bring in more advertising, and make more money.

It has taken me many years to understand the true impact of this and to understand how for so much of my journalism career, I accepted old conventions and bought into the narrative that objectivity was rooted in motivations that were noble. I'm not implying that well-intentioned journalists were somehow being disingenuous. With the benefit of hindsight and history, I am asserting that objectivity as a concept was and remains disingenuous.

The casual callousness of the killing of George Floyd and the sheer incompetence of the police in the killing of Breonna Taylor broke the dam, and their deaths hit me deeply.

I no longer could abide being objective, as if I had ever been. As the protests of 2020 exploded and signs signaling the value of Black lives began to be pinned to doors and windows in hoods and hamlets across the nation, there was a parallel movement emerging that was unlike any I had seen in my 20 years in journalism. It was long overdue.

The call to arms was simple and profound: dismantle systemic racism in news.

We are finally saying what needs to be said about mainstream American journalism: that much of it has perpetuated systemic racism and sheltered White supremacy, and for mainstream journalism to survive with any shred of credibility, it must be held accountable, rehabilitated, and reimagined.

It has taken a two decades-long journey that has woven through many journalistic roles, experiences, lessons, and projects to wash up on a new beach of journalistic views and values.

In 2010, while serving as managing editor at the *Tribune,* I started a program called Oakland Voices, which was inspired in part by a convening I attended, put on by Journalism That Matters (JTM), a group of disaffected journalists seeking a better way.

The group reminded me of that show, *Kung Fu*, in which David Carradine stars as the mixed-race "Shaolin monk and martial arts expert Caine, who fled China after his master was killed. He wandered the Old West of America trying to find his half-brother and seeking to defend the helpless" as one description of the show put it. JTM resembled the wanderings of Caine as the group sought to find a new, more meaningful path for its sacred craft.

I had forgotten that the character of Caine was actually mixed race in the show, which wasn't something I recall seeing much of on TV during the early 1970s. Carradine himself was not mixed race; he was White, and I can imagine by today's standards that casting him as the lead would be seen as unacceptable, viewed as another example of cultural appropriation and erasure of Chinese and Asian culture.

At the time I became aware of the show (which aired between 1972-1975), I would have been about 8 or 10 years old. I was taken aback by the unique nature of the storyline, its pacing, and that there was not a lot of fighting or violence. Caine rarely used his martial arts gifts, opting for the teachings of his temple to resolve and navigate conflict.

I was managing editor at the *Tribune* between 2005 and 2007 before becoming editor in chief in 2008. I recall beginning to feel that journalism needed to move with a different pace, in a more collaborative and less confrontational way when engaging in the coverage of regular folks—not politicians, officials, or public figures—and when covering certain topics and communities.

I knew at the time that the *Tribune* was losing or had lost relationships with parts of the community in Oakland. It needed to rebuild and reconnect, and a group of residents and I were invited to a conference that helped us envision what might be possible.

Out of that experience, and with the help of this group of Oakland folks, I developed an idea to create a program that would train residents to become storytellers. They would write stories the *Tribune* would never think to do, or whenever possible, write stories that could augment coverage the paper was doing. To top it off, we would house the program inside a space at one of the branches of the Oakland Public Library.

The Maynard Institute, where I now work and colead the organization with Evelyn Hsu, helped develop the curriculum and structure of the program, and we got money from the California Endowment to do it. Dori Maynard, a dear friend, journalist, and former president of the institute, along with Hsu, were instrumental in bringing this project to fruition.

And my bosses at the time, vice president of news for Bay Area News Group, Kevin Keane, and Bay Area news group managing editor, Pete Wevurski, didn't take much convincing—even though it was something completely different from anything we had ever done and was among the first-ever programs of its kind with a mainstream news outlet as a partner.

Gerry Garzon (who was number two at the Oakland Public Library) and his boss were supportive and rented space to us in the West Oakland branch to house the program. We started a community newsroom.

Journalism should be collaborative and cocreated with community. . . . We see an exciting emergence of community-centered models that have fully embraced this.

We advertised the program, residents applied, and we had *Tribune* reporters, photographers, and editors help teach classes. Each correspondent was to do 10 stories over nine months. We replicated the program in Jackson, Mississippi, and in Sacramento, California. The Oakland program has now entered its 13th year and has graduated dozens of correspondents, some of whom have gone on to write professionally and still contribute to the program today as alumni.

The conversations with residents and the folks at JTM, plus my own orientation to lean toward community, taught me that journalism should be collaborative and cocreated with community. My thinking on this was not as clear as it is today, and we see an exciting emergence of community-centered models that have fully embraced this. I would like to think Oakland Voices played a part in helping this trend emerge and for it to be seen as a pioneer in the space.

We kept evolving the program as my roles changed in the organization. I became the first community engagement editor for Bay Area News

Group, which further informed my thinking about community storytelling in collaboration with news outlets.

I will admit that the piece about racial justice had not emerged in my thinking about this, although it was implicit in the communities we wanted to reach. Also, the Maynard Institute's Fault Lines framework was infused in the conception of the program. That framework was developed by Robert C. Maynard—one of the nine founders of the institute, former editor and publisher of the *Oakland Tribune*, and the first African American to own and operate a major metropolitan newspaper—in collaboration with his wife, Nancy Hicks Maynard, a prolific journalist and leader in her own right.

Robert Maynard talked about how five (now six) social fault lines— race, class, gender, generation, geography, and sexual orientation— and the fissures of politics, religion, and ability are among the deepest tension points in our society. And how we align across these social fault lines affects how we see the world.

During this time, I was on the board of the institute. After Dori Maynard passed, the institute was having a challenging time navigating the changes across journalism. I left Bay Area News Group in 2015 to help Evelyn Hsu reimagine the organization. I joined as a strategic planning fellow, and with funding from the John S. and James L. Knight Foundation and Ford Foundation, we undertook a planning process that helped rethink and refocus the institute.

Programs such as the Maynard 200 Fellowship emerged from this process. It is a fellowship program that focuses on journalism entrepreneurship, executive leadership, storytelling (a term pulled directly from Oakland Voices), and most recently, mid-level managers and editors.

Throughout all this work, we hadn't yet landed on calling for dismantling systemic racism in news. However, while I conducted Fault Lines diversity training sessions in newsrooms, I always thought something was missing in the conversation, but it wasn't until early 2020 that the missing piece came into focus.

In June of that year, I was part of a University of Southern California Annenberg Center for Health Journalism panel that focused on how journalists could care for themselves during the height of the protests.[4]

One of the panelists, Dr. Glenda Wrenn, talked about people needing to ask themselves, "Are you going to be sustainers, creators, deniers, facilitators, or dismantlers of systemic racism?"

"Wow," I thought to myself, "This is something journalists and news organizations (as well as foundations and academic institutions) need to be asking."

At the very least, mainstream news organizations have been sustainers and facilitators of systemic racism and White supremacy culture. One example that can be pointed to is the coverage of crime in the printed product, on news websites, and local television newscasts. How often did outlets run police mugshots full of Black and Brown faces knowing they drive page views and drive ratings?

News organizations have cocreated with police departments, giving their reports and quotes more weight than they would the account of a person from the community. We regularly approached coverage this way during my years at the *Tribune* because the police at least had a professional obligation to be accountable for on-the-record statements. Simultaneously, we would subject community accounts to a kind of silent scrutiny because, we posited, folks on the street have no obligation to tell the truth. Given what we know about police reports and accounts of police violence made by police, officers have shown themselves to hold no more of an obligation for truth than anyone else, but they are given the benefit of the doubt by many in power that they will be truthful.

There has been a shift away from the ubiquitous use of mug shots and police blotters that lack context, over-index communities of color, and ignore systemic racism in law enforcement. Nonjournalists would likely be surprised at how recent some of those moves have been and how pervasive shoddy crime coverage—particularly on local television news broadcasts—continues to be.

Earlier in this piece, I noted the journalistic *mea culpas* of some newspapers that have apologized for racist coverage. As important as those apologies might be, an apology isn't accountability.

The *Baltimore Sun* did lay out the actions it was taking to address its failures, which included developing a diverse source database, building a style guide, nurturing the pipeline of talent, forming outreach committees, and working with the Maynard Institute on a content audit and diversity training for the staff.

Mainstream outlets have often reported on systems, such as education or health care, from the perspective of what is, not from what must be dismantled from the ground up. Many have called for the burning down of mainstream news organizations, but I want to ask you, What could emerge from the ashes of those fires? What is possible? What is the dream?

And while mainstream journalism seeks to speak truth to power, whose truth are they speaking?

We also talk a lot in our profession about holding power to account. Who is holding us accountable? How are we holding ourselves accountable?

Writing about the problems of a system isn't the same as calling for the complete dismantling of it. And I wonder how internalized White supremacy on the part of those in journalism affects the approach to coverage. Clearly, there has been some recognition that harm has been done, but I am curious just how deep certain outlets are willing to go to truly account for the pain they have caused and the invisibility they have perpetuated on individual journalists and on many different constituencies.

What we saw during the summer of 2020 was a racial reckoning that exploded in the streets, and its shockwaves were felt within newsrooms across the country. A new generation of journalists no longer saw themselves as separate from these killings. They saw themselves in Floyd, in Taylor, and could no longer bifurcate the stories from their lived experiences. I, too, saw myself in Floyd, in Taylor, and in the faces of countless other people of color who had been slain by police.

It was profound, and it was time to go even further in analyzing what journalism must aspire to if it is to heal the harm it has caused and to be seen as worthy of the privilege of informing a diverse nation and world. Out of the decades of pain, exclusion, and toxicity, we at the Maynard Institute have landed on an aspiration that could help heal the wounds journalism has so carelessly inflicted on so many people of color: belonging.

My Own Story of Belonging

Many may not know of my life as a musician and lyricist. I played trumpet for many years and later picked up a microphone as hip-hop was emerging in the mid- to late-1980s. Even as an intern and young reporter at the *Tribune*, I was in bands that traveled to western Europe, Cuba, and around the United States. I performed with artists such as Joshua Redman, Christian McBride, Carlos Santana, and the Wu-Tang Clan, among others. Being a lyricist helped me become a better journalist, and being a journalist helped me become a better songwriter. It wasn't until I became managing editor of the *Oakland Tribune* in 2005 that I set my music aspirations aside to focus on leading the newspaper I had grown to love.

But the lessons I learned as a member of one band in particular never left me. In the mid-1990s, I was part of a group called Mingus Amungus,[5] a Charles Mingus[6] tribute band dedicated to reimagining the music of the legendary jazz bassist and composer. In this band were traditional jazz musicians, dancers, and lyricists, each trying to bring their unique talents to the stage. We all had to find our way. As part of the group, there were those who didn't listen to jazz, and those who didn't listen to hip-hop, but all had to play in support of each other on stage. There was immense creative tension within the group because people needed to bring their authentic selves to the music, and, because of the diversity of the members, it was challenging. There were generational, racial, gender, class, and geographical fault lines at play all the time!

In many ways, the band reminded me of a news organization. People brought a mix of perspectives, talents, technology, and leadership to the group. It was often hard and frustrating to get jazz musicians who didn't understand the complex simplicity of hip-hop rhythms to respect what was needed to bring my contribution to its fullest potential. It required compromise, clarity, leadership, patience, and a willingness to learn—from all of us.

The result onstage was a band that was dynamic and award-winning; it provided an experience that people had never before seen. We were all pushing to belong, much like what we are seeing now in news organizations.

When you belong, you can bring your whole self to your work and the result is profound. When you belong, you can use phrases like "home going" to describe a funeral and not be looked at sideways by an editor who doesn't understand. When you belong, you can feel it in your bones. You can feel it in the fact that you're not the only one of you. It can be seen, as journalist Michelle Garcia said, through the shifting of the journalistic gaze, away from Whiteness, to the kaleidoscope of gazes that reflect our society and our world.

When you belong, you can feel it in your bones.

You can just be.

I conduct diversity and other related training for news organizations all around the country. They are for-profit, nonprofit, and corporate-owned, as well as start-ups and so-called legacy institutions. Print, digital, broadcast, public media . . . all of it.

The thread that stitches their struggles together is the same thread that weaves its way through our nation's fabric: racism, sexism, misogyny, patriarchy, and White supremacy culture are all present to some degree or another.

So often, there is an ambient racism that hangs in the air at even the most progressive of news outlets. It is in those places where the racism can be the most insidious because there is a false fragrance of "not possible here because we're good people" that is dangerous and disingenuous.

Despite what lingers, it feels as though the soil has been turned across the field of journalism.

It has been unearthed by the demographic shifts illustrated in the 2020 Census, made all the more powerful by a March 10 news report that revealed that the US Census Bureau disproportionately undercounted Hispanic, Black, and Native American residents.[7] According to a story in the *New York Times*, bureau officials assert the overall population total was accurate but that counts of minorities were skewed. Advocacy groups threatened to go to court.

Even with the skewed numbers, the data are undeniable. This country is changing; it *has* changed.

It is Browner and more diverse than ever. The violence we see against communities of color is not sustainable if we are going to be a healthy and whole nation. News organizations can't stop this violence. But they can stop perpetuating their own version of violence by not turning a blind eye to newsroom cultures that are toxic and harmful.

A delicious irony has emerged in that many White people, who have enjoyed living in a country where they haven't had to account for their Whiteness, are beginning to feel a sense that in many parts across this land, they don't belong. Or that the belonging they have taken for granted is somehow being infringed upon by those who don't look like them.

How will news organizations respond to this increasing sentiment?

(Particularly when so many are ill equipped, too hasty, and too stressed to even have a conversation about these issues among themselves, let alone have the skill and ability to engage with communities of color who represent the audiences of the future.)

Part of creating a culture of belonging is slowing down long enough to realize and embrace that there are differing paces and rhythms to how people move. What might it look like for mainstream outlets that seek to serve broad audiences to develop a level of cultural sophistication that enables the journalists in them to move and operate in a way that is natural to their cultural experience? How powerful would it be for an outlet to make that a strategic pillar of success and develop coverage, engagement, hiring, and business practices to reflect that approach? How amazing would that be?

> Part of creating a culture of belonging is slowing down long enough to realize and embrace that there are differing paces and rhythms to how people move.

I am seeking to connect with and better understand my own privilege. I am Black, biracial, male, middle class, educated, and colead an organization that is respected. This collection of elements affords me a measure of influence, comfort, and confidence that must be appreciated and reflected on. How has socialized patriarchy influenced the way I move and interact with colleagues? What must

I account for and be sensitive to when interacting with different people of different backgrounds and across fault lines?

I am seeking to be more intentional, more careful, and more accommodating in service of being in community. And I make mistakes all the time. I am learning, growing, and so often the journey is damn uncomfortable . . . and I do this work for a living!

It's difficult to be in community if you see yourself apart from it, which is so often the approach that mainstream journalism takes.

I encourage all journalists to embrace their own work to unwind bias and internalized White supremacy or patriarchy. The toil of that process is even more necessary than learning how to crunch numbers in a data set or file a Freedom of Information Act request.

Slow down. Become less extractive in your asks of community and of sources that are not official or familiar with the news media. Do your own internal work as you do the work of journalism. Do less extraction and more investment. We must offer authentic humility and care.

And there is another part to all of this that underpins being a person of color working in journalism.

Karena H. Montag is a psychotherapist and cofounder of Stronghold, a nonprofit collective that works to embed restorative and racial justice into organizations.[8]

While at lunch some months ago, she spoke about the concern she has for her Black son, who is living in and navigating a society that is designed to kill or imprison him. If he rises too high, steps out too far, he could be at risk. "How do you shine and survive?" she asked.

Her words struck me. They blew me over like a ship on its keel.

As we push for a kind of journalistic liberation, to belong, to rise and shine, how will people, who happen to be journalists of color, LGBTQ+, or of diverse levels of physical ability, survive?

As we seek to be seen, to no longer be invisible, what might be the risks to our safety and our sanity?

Survive the streets.
Survive the police.

How will we survive in newsrooms where people are actively or unconsciously trying to undermine or destroy us?

These are the questions journalism must ask itself and to reconcile if we are ever to be truly fit to serve this democracy.

Public-Powered Journalism

by Jennifer Brandel

I believe journalism plays an outsized role in determining whether American democracy flat out fails or evolves to meet the needs of the current complex context. Journalism is many things at once: an industry, a practice, a bogeyman, and a system through which to create sense-making, belonging, and collective action. Because of the many ways journalism is woven into the fabric of democracy, I find it impossible to separate it out completely from the threads of business, governance, public health, and culture and examine it as though it's a stand-alone object. Regardless, journalism is not working as it should—at least for most people.

So, what I've been endeavoring to do in my career is to tease out some of the myriad problems with current journalistic practices and incentive structures to replace what's been frayed with stronger, more durable approaches that can reinforce a healthier democracy.

Of the various initiatives I've started, there are dozens that have petered out or whose time has not yet come. So what I'll share here are those that are in motion, along with others that I believe will be operative relatively soon, and how they relate to journalism and the health of democracy.

Each of these initiatives has come about through relationships with other thinkers, practitioners, and contacts with organizations who are game to test out new ideas and learn together. Every subsequent intervention was born from bumping up against the limitations of a system and the need to create new rules to break through.

Public-Powered Journalism

In 2012, I had an opportunity through a unique collaboration started by the Association of Independents in Radio (AIR) to conduct a yearlong editorial experiment. I applied for AIR's Localore program with an idea that came to me after working for the Bahá'í faith for a few years. Though I'm not Bahá'í myself, I am fascinated by the religion and how it approaches the work of strengthening and improving communities and honoring the dignity and wisdom of individuals. Bahá'í is organized through a worldview that we are all members of one human family and that we are all experts in what we need through our own lived experience. Members of the faith do not approach a community with the idea that they have all the answers. They do not proselytize. Rather, they approach others in a posture of learning, listening to what people need, and asking how they can be of service.

This is the opposite of how most institutions, including those in journalism, operate. Journalists and editors work from the assumption that *they* know what the public needs to know and that it's their job to determine what's important to tell the public. This is despite the fact that no newsroom mirrors the demographics of the communities they serve and that journalists are not mind readers. I wondered: What if, instead of assuming that they already know what people are curious about and what information they need, journalists would start by asking them?

This simple idea—of giving the public power over the coverage they receive through the act of starting with their questions—was one that gave me quite a burst of energy. Having worked as a freelancer for newsrooms, I was always bothered by how much power I had to shape the narratives that hundreds of thousands of people were exposed to without first knowing if what I was reporting was actually useful to them. I was also flummoxed by how a newsroom could essentially operate as an autocracy and serve a democracy. Autocracies are governed by a very small group of people operating in a closed system, who make decisions for a very large group of people outside of their system. The power imbalance in newsrooms seemed profound, and this walling off of decision-making power from those whom those decisions ultimately impact felt like a real shortcoming. If journalism was to achieve its promise of creating the conditions for an informed and empowered citizenry, it seemed clear to me that those conditions would have to change.

> Journalists and editors work from the assumption that *they* know what the public needs to know and that it's their job to determine what's important to tell the public.

Curious City is the name of the news-gathering experiment I started in 2012 at WBEZ Chicago to test a more public-powered methodology. A small but mighty team consisting of a reporter/producer (me), an editor (Shawn Allee), and an intern (Logan Jaffe) began to source the ideas for our journalism outside of our editorial room and our own heads. We started by asking the public, "What do you wonder about Chicago, the region, or its people that you'd like WBEZ to investigate?" We did this in a variety of ways, including pounding the pavement with a microphone, launching custom-built surveys, and even a call-in number to leave questions for the newsroom. We then collected their responses, curating lists of questions that were related by tone, scope, or difficulty in reporting and let the public ultimately vote to decide what we spent our time reporting on. We did this through an online tool we developed that enabled visitors to the WBEZ site to cast one vote per voting round. We introduced this voting process—another democratic intervention—to make the process of journalism better reflect the system we were trying to operate within. Then, we invited the person whose question we were answering to be part of the storytelling. This meant that we opened up the mysterious and often idiosyncratic process of gathering information and shaped it through outside input and opinion.

Ultimately, we found that the stories created through this process were noticeably *better* than the stories we reported through the traditional process of a small, homogeneous group of people pitching a story, an editor assigning it, and a reporter deciding what information should be gathered and written up—all out of sight from the public they're serving. These public-powered stories were more original—there were no other news outlets in town doing this same story. Our stories often broke news because they drew on observations that weren't otherwise known to a reporter. And they centered on the public, rather than on people in power, in determining why the story should even exist in the first place. All these stories were asked for by the public, not bequeathed to them by newsroom assumptions. It turns out that reporters also felt more fulfilled by reporting these stories because they knew that these stories mattered. They didn't have to guess whether people cared about the topic because people in the community had chosen it in the first place.

Within the first year of Curious City's life, other newsrooms started contacting me to better understand what it was that made our approach different and how they could launch a similar intervention in their own newsrooms to make their editorial process more democratic.

After hearing from a dozen or so newsrooms, I decided that my time could best be spent trying to answer the question, Is the public-powered process replicable and repeatable? I wondered if I could help more newsrooms become more democratic by supporting them in testing and gaining confidence in the public-powered process.

These public-powered stories were more original—there were no other news outlets in town doing this same story.

While I had initially hoped to be able to answer that question while continuing my work at WBEZ, it became clear that this project was beyond the scope of the station's particular mission for serving Chicago (and not the whole news ecosystem). I've found this to be a constant battle for systems thinkers and builders; we have to find containers that allow for the expansion of emergent insights. Most organizations are not able to accommodate emergence, so we need to either start our own more flexible companies or live our lives in a somewhat scattered way doing work across a variety of organizations.

Thanks to some financial support to scale the public-powered concept, I stepped away from WBEZ in late 2014 and started a company called Hearken in 2015. (Curious City is ongoing and celebrated its 10th year in production in 2022.)

Hearken to Hearken

The word *hearken* means "to listen," which felt like the perfect name for a company that's rooted in listening. Hearken has been focused since 2015 on helping other organizations (mostly those in the journalism industry) operate more democratically by opening their closed processes to outsiders. We've seen that for newsrooms to be successful, they need more than the philosophy: they need the technology to help them operationalize the practice and make it part of their routines. They also need consulting support to help them get over the inevitable challenges of thinking in a new way and not returning to the status quo.

One of the major problems we've come across in working with newsrooms is that often their routines are still rooted in the machine age—a time when there was information scarcity and newsrooms competed with one another to be the go-to source for truth about "what's happening." Prior to the digital age, it made sense for newsrooms to optimize for speed, efficiency, and distribution. After all, they were in a market of information scarcity, so hustling to get their information out as soon as possible in whatever formats were available (i.e., TV, radio, and newspapers) was how they judged their success and built their economic models. This operating system is the one in which journalists, editors, and producers are charged with "feeding the beasts," that is, every day they go to work knowing they need to produce a certain amount of content for whatever container they're working in (e.g., a broadcast clock or newspaper column length).

Though the public has been completely oversaturated with information for decades, the incentives driving journalists to create as much content as possible and as quickly as possible persist. Imagine if, instead, journalists were incentivized to support collective sense-making, or to distribute the responsibility for care within a community, or to provide a forum for people to find common ground and other like-minded people to take civic action? The industry would need to change on fundamental levels.

At Hearken we've noticed newsrooms that have acknowledged we're now in the information age are becoming less fixated on producing as much content as quickly as possible. Instead, they're optimizing for relevance, trust, and service. In today's low-trust environment, rife with misinformation, it does not matter whether you're producing incredible content if there's no public that trusts your news outlet enough to even receive it. In this context, public engagement in the editorial process and the public-powered journalism model I started testing at WBEZ become assets.

We've found that newsrooms with journalists who listen to and involve the public in their editorial decisions report that their stories land better with the publics they already serve and get further out to audiences they haven't yet reached. There are a number of reasons for this. One thing journalists can take for granted is that it's exciting for people to be in the news (when it's for a good reason). When journalists involve and credit the person whose question or information needs catalyzed a story and name them in the story—be that on video, in an online article, on a podcast, or in another product—that person is highly motivated to share with his or her circles. And when their circles learn their friend is in the news, they're likewise inspired to pay more attention to that media outlet and to that issue—perhaps even to the extent of becoming involved themselves. In this process, the public helps to identify and shape an understanding of the issue, which can then encourage greater participation in creating potential solutions.

As noted above, these stories and this model can drive economic wins for newsrooms as well. Our aim is to help more and more newsrooms realize that by failing to involve the public in a meaningful way in editorial decision-making, they're losing out on a number of major benefits that can help them meet this moment and sustain their businesses. But transitioning from the mindset of optimizing for speed and distribution, rather than for relevance and trust, is extremely difficult in a business that's focused on deadlines and short-term thinking.

> When . . . news organizations belong to the people they are meant to serve, the incentives . . . will have ripple effects on editorial planning, collaborative reporting, and financial sustainability.

Trying to build Hearken into a company for the long-term by relying on newsrooms to make this paradigm shift quickly—and paying us for our services—was a major stumbling block and pointed the way to the next intervention I needed to create.

Zebras Unite

Without inserting a 10,000-word treatise on the foundations of capitalism and the realities of start-up culture circa the early 2000s, suffice it to say that I've found starting a company as a woman and looking for aligned capital to grow it have been nearly impossible.

Zebras Unite is a founder-led, cooperatively owned movement creating the culture, capital, and community for the next economy. Here's how it got its start: in 2016, I coauthored an essay called "Sex & Startups" with a dear friend and fellow start-up entrepreneur, Mara Zepeda, who is the founder of Switchboard. We articulated the difficulty of starting and sustaining mission-based, for-profit companies such as ours that can scale up and the lack of capital for companies that don't fit the Silicon Valley model (so-called unicorn companies valued at over a billion dollars). Zebras are companies that balance profit and purpose and see collaboration, not competition, as core to their survival. Since 2016, we've taken this idea and the energy it released and spun it into a multistakeholder cooperative and a 501(c)(3). We have chapters around the world, a community of thousands of entrepreneurs and investors, and we are working to create the culture, capital, and community necessary to support the types of businesses we believe will be needed for the complex problems the 21st century portends.

Just as the public-powered model of journalism subverts the autocracy of newsroom editorial decision-making, Zebras Unite subverts the autocracy of funding. Typically, new companies have to find start-up capital through investors or banks—which tend to be small groups of people who do not demographically represent the people seeking funding. The statistics for getting capital are abysmal for companies started by women and people of color. But through pioneering different funding and lending models such as the Inclusive Capital Collective, Zebras Unite is creating new processes and vehicles for finding aligned capital.

We're also working to understand how cooperative ownership structures can align with the needs and goals of news organizations. We are working with the Media Enterprise Design Lab (MEDLab) at the University of Colorado Boulder, which is a think tank for community ownership and governance in media organizations. We collaborated with them on a new model to help the owners of start-ups think not about an "exit" (sale) to the highest-paying investor in order to make a lot of money, but instead "exiting to community" and selling ownership to the people you're serving. Out of these conversations sprang a special group that's working to apply cooperative models to news start-ups. We believe that when the ownership and governance of news organizations belong to the people they are meant to serve, the incentives become powerfully aligned and will have ripple effects on editorial planning, collaborative reporting, and financial sustainability. Instead of newsrooms needing to answer to advertisers, hedge funds, or investors to be paid, they'll need to answer to the people whom they're designing their reporting to serve.

Given the learning that happens when ambitious, community-centric entrepreneurs start newsrooms with a new model and the fact that the field of investment capital is rapidly changing to become more impact-oriented, I expect that, in a few years, there will be far more diverse paths for those who want to start such news organizations. Further, they will be able to find the seed funding to get them off the ground so that they eventually can be owned and operated by the community.

To me, this is the biggest and most important shift that can happen for the media. It's not immediate; it's not going to fix the misinformation crisis, nor will it stanch the bleeding of newsroom layoffs, consolidations, and shutdowns. But just adding more journalists to newsrooms that are built on broken business models and financial incentives will definitely not help support people in communities doing the work of addressing the shared problems that threaten our democracy.

The Citizens Agenda

As I've sought to create frameworks, processes, technology, and culture around listening and decentralized decision-making, I've found additional ways to extend these concepts and apply them to journalism. I want to talk now explicitly about democracy.

While it's become clear to newsrooms in the past few years that listening and engaging with the people they serve is essential to their relevance and survival, still, we find imaginations are limited in newsrooms for how they can pull away from the feeding-the-beast mentality of churning out content. This inertia becomes especially dangerous when applied to one of the most important functions journalism can play in a democracy: to help people understand what's at stake in an election and to help them make informed choices when casting their ballots.

In 2019, media critic and scholar Jay Rosen was in Chicago and stopped by the Hearken offices. We got to talking about his Citizens Agenda approach, a reporting framework that starts with what the public wants politicians to talk about as they compete for votes. It is essentially public-powered journalism applied to the election beat. We decided to collaborate so we could operationalize the Citizens Agenda and help newsrooms with a step-by-step guide to using this approach for covering the 2020 elections.

This movement to make the Citizens Agenda easier for newsrooms to follow became the catalyst for an even bigger intervention we created around the 2020 elections.

Election SOS

Hearken used its own listening approach and asked, "What do journalists wonder as they approach the 2020 elections?" Newsrooms knew that the ground had shifted since the election of Donald Trump and understood that the way they'd covered the 2016 elections was not a good match for the times. But what to do instead was still a matter of much debate.

Hearken heard from many journalists about the needs they had: They needed specific training in how to apply the Citizens Agenda, they needed support for increasing their trust in the public, and they needed targeted training about how to recognize and handle emergent threats to a successful election (e.g., disinformation, White nationalism and violence, voter suppression, COVID-19 and vote-by-mail protocols). In collaboration with the American Press Institute and Trusting News, Hearken launched a pop-up collaborative called Election SOS. It included not only targeted resources and training, but also fellowships and grants to directly support newsrooms in responding quickly to urgent needs.

Election SOS was very successful by every metric we established. We served thousands of journalists, trained and deployed fellows, and disbursed hundreds of thousands of dollars in grants, but, of course, the threats that existed during the 2020 election have not gone away. So, in 2021, we launched the Democracy SOS fellowship, which builds off the lessons learned from Election SOS. Hearken and the Solutions Journalism Network are partnering to bring our "best of" training modules into a long-term fellowship program, which started by focusing on the 2022 elections while also deepening the potential for change in how journalists approach their work and how newsrooms operate.

Specifically, we created a training module about *high conflict*, a term that refers to discord that develops into a good-versus-evil kind of feud that fans the flames of polarization. This module is designed to help journalists better understand how their reporting practices can—and often do—exacerbate high conflict and undermine democracy in the process. We're interested in naming and reframing the role journalism plays in democracy, in equipping practitioners with an understanding of how they create harm, and in learning how to mitigate that harm through their practices. For instance, we know that presenting only two sides to a story creates a binary "us vs. them" narrative that encourages black-and-white thinking and leads to further polarization.

We're learning that to help inspire changes in journalistic practices to support democracy, we need a mixture of short-term incentives and long-term support for paradigmatic change. The Democracy SOS fellowship used the short-term need to supply better coverage for the 2022 midterms as a training ground for deploying different practices that will support trust-building with the American public and directly serve their information needs.

The Future Is in Decentralized Decision-Making

You're probably sensing a theme to the interventions I'm drawn to creating: it's about ensuring that the power to decide is distributed and that the people who stand to be most affected by the decisions need to be involved in either creating the choices people are deciding between or shaping them so that the outcomes will be useful, relevant, and will inflict the least amount of harm. This thesis is not something I consciously set out to work with; it's only in looking back at my body of work that I see it's the central value amid all my various companies, projects, and initiatives. In considering democracy as a system of governance in which decentralized decision-making forms the foundation of how a society functions within and outside of a geographic territory, I think any way that journalism can support better listening and decentralized decision-making within its practice and within the communities in which it operates, the better chance our democracy has at survival.

> Any way that journalism can support better listening and decentralized decision-making within its practice . . . the better chance our democracy has at survival.

For journalism to better inform people doing the work of supporting democracy, the industry must start seeing itself and acting as part of a larger, decentralized network of the civic body, rather than as a siloed industry. It must see that the information it provides is just one stream in the larger flow of information that supports collective sense-making. And journalists must appreciate that some of the solutions required to improve the health of our democracy are in their hands.

I don't know that I'll see the change toward healthier newsrooms and a thriving media ecosystem to support democracy within my lifetime, but my hope is that at least one (or more) of the interventions I've been fortunate enough to build and deploy thus far, results in some noticeable and useful change.

Working *with* the Community

by Ben Trefny

On Tuesday, November 8, 2016, I anchored KALW Public Radio's live election night coverage. As host, I broke the news that Donald Trump would be the next president of the United States. One of my guests, dumbfounded, said, "I feel like a stranger in my own country." I contemplated that and responded, "Clearly a lot of people already did."

Trump's election shocked many journalists. Massive investments in polling and analysis had missed the mark. Anticipating the election of Hillary Clinton to the presidency, the media narrative had typically discarded Trump as a serious candidate while simultaneously capitalizing on his celebrity to draw audiences to their own outlets. At the same time, journalists had failed to reflect enough upon what stories might be missing—and upon the perception audiences might have about the storytellers and their agendas. In fact, Trump's election resulted in part from the public's well-documented dissipating trust in the institution of journalism itself.[1]

American mainstream media has traditionally served certain (wealthier and Whiter) audiences while leaving out or *othering* some audiences (poorer and people of color) entirely. There are many excuses.

For example, journalism is dependent on paymasters. It's also in an existential economic crisis.[2] This manifests itself, particularly for the biggest outlets with the most journalists, in a drive to attract the largest possible audience. In commercial media, operational revenue is driven by advertising dollars. In noncommercial media, larger audience numbers translate to more donations.

The bottom line, then, comes down to demographics and how to appeal to the masses.

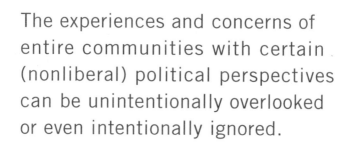

The experiences and concerns of entire communities with certain (nonliberal) political perspectives can be unintentionally overlooked or even intentionally ignored.

In racial terms, 61.6 percent of the US population is White alone.[3] White people are not monolithic, but when an institution is dependent on appealing to that demographic, editorial choices are made to meet the audience's perceived interests.

Of course, as many journalists would note, it's not that simple (or that cynical). Editorial and financial departments typically have firewalls in place to ensure journalistic integrity. And yet the leaders at most major news organizations are also White,[4] which impacts the choices that are made about what to cover and how to cover it. The stories of mainstream journalism are told through a White filter.

One other wrinkle is the sensibility of these decision makers. The *Columbia Journalism Review* wrote about this just over a decade ago:

> The mainstream press is liberal. Once, before 1965, reporters were a mix of the working stiffs leavened by ne'er-do-well college grads unfit for corporate headquarters or divinity school. Since the civil rights and women's movements, the culture wars and Watergate, the press corps at such institutions as the *Washington Post*, ABC-NBC-CBS News, the *NYT*, the *Wall Street Journal*, *Time*, *Newsweek*, the *Los Angeles Times*, the *Boston Globe*, etc. is composed in large part of "new" or "creative" class members of the liberal elite—well-educated men and women who tend to favor abortion rights, women's rights, civil rights, and gay rights. In the main, they find such figures as Bill O'Reilly, Glenn Beck, Sean Hannity, Pat Robertson, or Jerry Falwell beneath contempt.[5]

Unless outlets directly address that discrepancy, it means that the experiences and concerns of entire communities with certain (nonliberal) political perspectives can be unintentionally overlooked or even intentionally ignored. Taken altogether, mainstream journalism, as an industry, is largely led by White, politically liberal people who are deeply concerned with their industry's survival and subsequently make choices that exclude entire segments of their potential audience.

What conclusion can we draw from all this? Despite what may be well-intentioned efforts, journalists often do not represent, nor are they in tune with, many people they are supposed to serve. So why would journalism be a trusted institution?

In a democracy, the people—all the people—are supposed to govern themselves. So, it fails when entire communities are misrepresented or excluded by those who wield power and influence. Journalism contributes to that failure. It has earned mistrust. Trump exploited that issue by *rightly stating* that journalists don't represent the interests of the people they say they're serving.

So how do journalists solve for that? In this essay, I'll discuss several efforts one news outlet—where I've worked for nearly two decades—has made to change its own narrative and literally connect *with* communities.

Before I go too far, I want to make sure to note, here, that I am a straight, cis, White man. I have a master's degree in journalism. I am the news director for KALW Public Media, serving the San Francisco Bay Area and producing journalistic podcasts with a national and international audience. I am also the president of the Northern California chapter of the Society of Professional Journalists. From an external perspective, and perhaps even an internal one, my identity and the fact that I hold such positions of authority can be seen as a fundamental problem. For some, that's inarguable. But I can say that my privileges have afforded me a firsthand view on a flawed industry filled with many people who want to do better. And I *can* speak to my team's efforts to do that.

In our news department, we identify ourselves as public-interest journalists, which means we're driven to serve people, not profits. We miss the mark all the time. But we reflect, we adapt, and we grow. What we've learned is that journalism is best practiced *with* the people in communities where we work.

Here's how.

The Sights and Sounds of Bayview

In 2013, early in Barack Obama's second term as president (and when I served as KALW's executive news editor under then-news director Holly Kernan), we partnered with the San Francisco Arts Commission to tell the stories of the people who live and work in San Francisco's Bayview neighborhood and those who positively affect it. The project was called "The Sights and Sounds of Bayview."[6] Radio producers and photographers documented the stories in sound and imagery. We communicated with community organizations, hired reporters to tell stories, and presented those pieces *live* on stage at the historic Bayview Opera House in front of an audience of local community members and newcomers to the neighborhood. It was a packed house, and many organizations set up tables around the room, showcasing what they do for their community.

Less than two years later, we applied for and received funding to hold another Sights and Sounds of Bayview event. But this one didn't go as well. We hired a community engagement producer, but he wasn't from the neighborhood and wasn't as successful making community connections. Our reporters told stories *about* the community but less in collaboration *with* the community. Also, significantly, the lovely community venue we'd booked for the previous show was being rehabilitated, so we had to hold our live event in an acoustically and visually unpleasant gymnasium. To make matters worse, out of our own ignorance, we scheduled it at the same time as a nearby outdoor block party. Altogether, the effort felt unsatisfying and disconnected from the community we were trying to serve.

While we certainly never intended it to come across as an out-of-touch project, it definitely resonated as a "White savior" effort. With the exception of our community engagement producer, our team members did not identify as people of color, and, for our audience, seeing our reporters on stage speaking about communities of color that they didn't know well outside of their reporting played poorly.

We learned lessons from that experience. We needed to work not just *for* people in a community, but in concert *with* them. (This is, of course, not our own exclusive idea; former Kettering Foundation President and CEO David Mathews[7] has written about the need for this across institutions in his book *With the People: An Introduction to an Idea.*[8]) Our journalists shouldn't have reported on locations as outsiders; they needed to invest time in the community getting to know people and issues for longer periods of time. And we needed community partners who would feel as invested in the reporting as we did and who would understand that we weren't just there as short-timers.

So, we looked to collaborate.

The Sights and Sounds of East Oakland

I attended a conference in 2015 where former *Oakland Tribune* editor in chief Martin Reynolds was speaking. He talked about Fault Lines—a practice of examining the preconceptions and prejudices journalists often harbor as they report on issues.[9] Reynolds was leading an organization called Oakland Voices, composed of people from East Oakland who wanted to tell stories about their community. Their stories would be edited and directed by a professional journalist.[10] It was an inspiring and empowering program. When I talked with him about the dilemmas we faced in trying to do our best community-centered work, we found alignment and agreed to partner.

We applied for and received funding from the California Arts Council through a grant called Creative California Communities. We would build programming within East Oakland, providing education, journalism, and live events in partnership with Oakland Voices, the Oakland Public Library, and other local organizations, including the East Oakland Youth Development Center (EOYDC) and the Eastside Arts Alliance. We made two key hires: two women from East Oakland who were committed to journalism and storytelling about the community. And we set to work.

> Certain communities are generally talked at, or talked about, by journalists.

We focused on interacting with people in East Oakland neighborhoods. We'd schedule live events at coffee shops and art galleries that would be publicized by local organizations, and our reporters would be part of the program. We'd present a multimedia version of their stories, and then bring them on stage to answer questions from the audience. These were regularly the most popular parts of the program, which is understandable when you recognize that certain communities are generally talked at, or talked about, by journalists. An information exchange is entirely different: it's a conversation that enriches both parties.

Ultimately, we came to realize that these efforts would mean we weren't reporting *on* a community. We were reporting *with* a community.

As part of that, we agreed to provide wrap-around journalistic services for participants in the Oakland Voices program. Photography, editing, production work, sound engineering would all be part of the package. In all honesty, training people with little to no experience in journalism is time consuming. But one of the remarkable occurrences, which I will always emphasize, is that we were not the only teachers. The community members taught us as well.

Let me give an example. One woman, Kat Ferreira, wanted to do a story about the aftermath of the Ghost Ship tragedy. The Ghost Ship was the name of a warehouse converted into an artist collective that doubled as a party space for ravers. The warehouse was located in Oakland's Fruitvale neighborhood, which is majority Latinx. The artists in the collective, however, were mostly White. One terrible night, the Ghost Ship caught fire during a party, and by the time it was over, 39 people had died. Ferreira wanted to see how this infamous event had impacted the neighborhood—a neighborhood that otherwise had very little to do with the people involved in the tragedy.

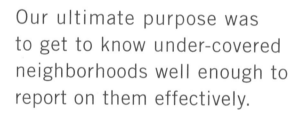

Our ultimate purpose was to get to know under-covered neighborhoods well enough to report on them effectively.

Ferreira wanted to talk with local residents, but she thought it would be a violation of their space and privacy to do so. She wanted to work out a strategy that wouldn't seem invasive. Her editor from KALW grew somewhat impatient with her hesitation and pushed for more aggressive reporting. Ultimately, Ferreira baked a batch of cookies to bring to her interview subjects, to be neighborly. She ended up getting the story—a nuanced perspective on how a community coped with death, public attention, and gentrification.[11]

Her story, however, came in later than expected, pushing back the project's timeline in ways that might be seen by others in the field as unprofessional. At the same time, Kat was unhappy about how more traditional journalists, like her editor, would have gone about the same assignment. This conflict led to the need for administrative intervention to assure both reporter and editor that they shared the goal of telling the most accurate and least exploitative story. Doing the right thing can be messy.

Now, I want to be straightforward with you. This multifaceted project in East Oakland was challenging, required a lot of coordination, cost a lot of time and money, and often felt unfruitful. But that's what you get when you're trying to build relationships where none had existed before. As journalists, we're building upon a legacy of institutional neglect and mistrust, and it takes time and commitment to reverse a tainted history.

In this case, our ultimate purpose was to get to know under-covered neighborhoods well enough to report on them effectively. The project had several facets. In addition to working with community journalists like Kat through Oakland Voices, we taught media production to middle school students at EOYDC. We held live poetry readings and art shows. We set up tables at events such as National Night Out to solicit questions we could report on. And with a community liaison and dedicated producer from East Oakland helping guide our work, we took on stories that made an impact in the community. One that particularly comes to mind was about a traffic accident that claimed the lives of a six-year-old and his mother. Our transportation reporter had gotten to know people in the neighborhood through Q and A sessions about transit planning at live community events, and he attended a rally calling attention to the dangerous street where the people had been killed. The insight he gained into what people wanted and needed, and the authentic feelings he amplified, helped lead to the installation of traffic signals at that location. This was community reporting making a measurable impact.

Now, I recognize that any reporter could cover a demonstration that's calling attention to a dangerous intersection and effect change. But when a reporter knows people in the neighborhood, understands the surrounding factors, economics, and politics, and can draw upon this knowledge base to add insight and nuance to a story, it has a better chance.

We won many regional journalism awards for our Sights and Sounds of East Oakland project, and we also received a national award for best sports reporting for a series largely told from the perspective of people living in East Oakland. Called *BOUNCE: The Warriors' Last Season in Oakland*, it was a 15-part podcast exploring how the Golden State Warriors' move from East Oakland across the bay to San Francisco was impacting the community.[12]

Ultimately, after three years developing relationships in East Oakland, our funding to focus there ran out. We retained an East Oakland reporter, but we were forced to abandon many of the other initiatives in which we'd invested. While we, our partners, and our collective audiences found tremendous value in that reporting, the economically depressed community couldn't sustain the costs of our project, and our paymasters decided their money could be better spent elsewhere.

The 2016 Election

While we progressed on our journalistic evolution, politics happened. In the run-up to the 2016 election, we worked with longtime journalist and tech innovator Subramaniam (Subbu) Vincent, who was developing some interactive, survey-oriented software for newsrooms. We were interested in learning what our audience wanted covered, and through Vincent's tool, we discovered they wanted clarity. In other words, cut through the political rhetoric and keep it simple. As a representative democracy, California turns over to voters many measures that elsewhere would be legislated. This is meant to empower the electorate, but because of political agendas, misinformation, and a sheer overload of information, it tends to result in a confused group of voters. As such, they sometimes don't vote in their own interest.

The 2016 election would include some 25 ballot measures and propositions for San Francisco voters. Party-affiliated voter guides and other partisan media outlets could provide recommendations, but we learned that people just wanted to know the basics: What does the proposition do? Who is for and against it? Why? And who has spent what money on the campaign?

From that feedback, we created "Election Briefs"—two-minute audio capsules based on the five journalistic *w*'s (who, what, where, when, and why) and how—told by a reporter in an engaging way and set by a sound engineer to a musical beat. We aired them regularly during KALW's broadcasts of NPR's *Morning Edition* and *All Things Considered*. They immediately proved popular, and our metrics measuring the number of listeners clicking on the accompanying web stories jumped as Election Day approached. Voters needed clear, nonpartisan information to help them fill out their ballots, and two-minute summaries were an economical way to learn. We also took those briefs and created simple voter information guides, which we distributed in regional libraries.

On election night, 2016, I hosted KALW's live coverage along with the editor in chief of the weekly *East Bay Express* and a reporter from the *San Francisco Public Press*. Pretty standard stuff, really: people who could analyze election issues from detached perspectives. We had several reporters and trainees in the field, and at that time, we felt as though we were comprehensively covering our region as well as we could.

> That navel-gazing . . . is indicative of the ignorance of the media when conversations are primarily with members of their own profession.

We recognized, later, that everybody we had scheduled to speak was a journalist. They were trained, educated, critical thinkers. But for the audience, it would be easy to see us as an exclusive group talking among ourselves, without the ability to relate to the real-world issues we were purporting to cover. That navel-gazing, hearing our own opinions on the election, is indicative of the ignorance of the media when conversations are primarily with members of their own profession. Neglecting the people journalists purport to serve led to Trump's election win that night. And because we at KALW weren't looking outward and paying enough attention to what the general population was thinking about, we were equally guilty of letting the public down.

As journalists striving to increase people's understanding of our world, we knew we had to improve our work. So, we tried another experiment, handing the microphone directly to the audience.

California Speaks

In general, the media in this country have been criticized for not reflecting the voices of all its people. As a news outlet operating in the San Francisco Bay Area, we recognize where we've been deficient: we don't hear enough of the perspectives of people living outside this predominantly urban, left-leaning part of the country. The result is what people have referred to as an information bubble, and it applies just as much to people of other political persuasions in other locations, perpetuated by social media feeds catering to their core interests and media that don't go far enough to express counter-perspectives.

We wanted to create a project that would build connections between people of different opinions. The project was called California Speaks, and it was conducted as part of a learning agreement with the Kettering Foundation. California Speaks consisted of a "question of the week" (broadcast on the radio, in social media, on websites, and in newsletters) and a collection of called-in responses from around the state, fitting news magazine time slots and shareable as a web or social post.

Questions we asked included:

- How do you feel about the legalization of adult-use recreational marijuana?
- Does sexual harassment affect your workplace? What's missing from the conversation?
- What would it take to get you into a driverless car?

Participants heard or saw the question each week and were invited to call a toll-free phone number where they could share and record their first names, locations, and responses. The California Speaks team constructed a weekly package containing representative answers and distributed the text and audio to participating outlets for publication and broadcast in two- or four-minute segments.

The program ran for about nine months, beginning exactly one year after the election of President Trump. Our most valuable takeaway from California Speaks was that while people may live in regions that sway toward one political party, their thoughts on more granular issues are very diverse. The news media seem to have a tendency to generalize popular opinion, placing groups in buckets that are easily sorted and digested. But the variety of responses we received showed that's oversimplifying how people think.

From calls we received, we found that a stoner may have significant concerns about marijuana-related DUIs. And a doctor can have strong misgivings about his complicity in prescribing opioids. We gained perspective on how reporters should be cognizant of how they stereotype and represent communities; communities are made up of individuals who all have the capacity to think independently— and often do.

We also learned that it takes many resources to make a project like this successful. Working with partner outlets takes a lot of time and requires a great deal of relationship maintenance. We initially looked at California Speaks as a great idea that others would want to join in on, and while that proved true, their commitment and attention to the details of the project, and what would make it successful, flagged regularly. Journalists are often well-intentioned, but they are also often overcommitted and under-resourced.

Projects such as California Speaks, therefore, would greatly benefit from elements that actually have nothing to do with journalism. They need community relations specialists who can talk with partners and follow up with participants. They need budgets to advertise across different media and get the concept in front of different people who are bombarded with information and opportunities. And they need regular investment to keep them going. In a noncommercial, low-resource outlet like KALW, it was not really possible to meet all those needs. With regular paid staff administering the details, relationships, and handling marketing, a project such as this could potentially grow and even reach the virality that could help it achieve the crossover communication to which it aspired.

It was a promising but incomplete experiment in community engagement and information sharing. With continued investment in outreach and personnel, a project such as California Speaks could connect exponentially more people and facilitate understanding across divides. I hope to revisit the project in a continued effort to build communication bridges.

The Pandemic and the 2020 Election

Fast-forward a couple of very challenging years for journalists.

When the pandemic shut down the Bay Area, we really leaned into community service journalism and utilizing the resources we had available—primarily people power and our various broadcast and online communications platforms. Funding from an organization called Renaissance Journalism helped us shore up our technical needs and jump-start work we wanted to direct toward the 2020 election.[13] That led to applying for further funding from the Trusted Elections Network[14] Fund of the American Press Institute.[15]

With that money, we planned to support precincts in five counties with the lowest voter turnout, including parts of Fairfield, Richmond, West Oakland, Bayview, and East Palo Alto, by connecting with residents directly. Activities included creating bilingual flyers with targeted elections coverage to hang on every door in each precinct; working with neighborhood organizations and networks to solicit election-related questions; reporting stories and conducting interviews to answer community queries; producing Election Briefs in English and Spanish about every statewide proposition and county ballot measure relevant to each precinct; convening virtual town halls to answer questions, conduct debates, combat disinformation, and share information about where and how to vote; and partnering with Spanish- and English-language outlets specific to each community to share and publicize content and events. We literally met people where they were, producing a wealth of digestible election-related material along with printed, nonpartisan, voter information guides that our news department delivered door-to-door.

We were able to direct funding to an editor covering the election and focus her efforts on community engagement. This was a great and powerful choice. Her work involved researching community organizations and journalists to identify and develop relationships with influencers in each precinct. She worked with eight KALW volunteers to develop information databases about these communities and identified partnership opportunities with media outlets and organizations working to inform communities on election issues. She spoke at several community forums, organized outreach efforts at several locations around the Bay Area, and coordinated many more volunteers to distribute voter information guides specific to those precincts door-to-door in what had been low-voter-turnout neighborhoods. She oversaw production of more than 40 Election Briefs,[16] which aired on KALW as well as in their own podcast feed. And she helped to book and interview several guests who work within low-voter-turnout communities.[17]

On Tuesday, November 3, 2020, I anchored KALW Public Radio's live election night coverage with our election engagement editor. We interviewed 16 people that night, including multilingual journalist partners, youth activists, public servants, and our own reporters assigned to cover grassroots issues throughout the region. It felt like a representation of the entire Bay Area, with stories told through a wide variety of voices, representing multiple generations, ethnicities, races, and political views. This is what we should have been doing all along. But it has taken a journey of trial and error over many years to get there.

I think our biggest takeaways from all these efforts is the significant power of partnering with other journalism organizations to leverage our work and the importance of connecting in a regular and thoughtful way with local organizations serving communities we also hope to serve. We have known the value of both of those efforts, but in the last few years, we've hired more specifically with that outreach work in mind, and I think it's resulted in some of our most impactful community-related reporting endeavors. We need to staff up with outreach specialists on a regular basis, not just when made possible through grants. It's challenging, but it's worth it.

Our journalism has evolved to become more inclusive. The work is not just an election year effort, but one that pays off continuously with a more informed and involved citizenry, which is fundamental to a thriving democracy. We've learned how to continually engage directly and impactfully with communities we serve. And we've learned to be an institution more consciously serving people.

Dialogue Journalism: Adapting to Today's Civic Landscape

by Eve Pearlman

Where I Come From

When I was in school at Northwestern University's Medill School of Journalism in the mid-1990s, I often felt at odds with the majority of my peers, those who believed that their work could be objective or neutral and that the words or videos they crafted could be definitive expressions of reality.

The idea that the work we produce is not informed by who we are, by our experiences, by our economic and geographic and racial backgrounds, has never sat well with me.

We are all products of culture and community and experience. Just look at clothing or language or religion or music or ideas about family and friendship and marriage and parenting, and education. We are all products of our life experiences. And we experience life and create journalistic content from the sum total of our beings. We are all exactly who we are.

I trace my earliest awareness of a disjuncture between official news and life as I experienced it to reading the local newspaper, the

Boulder Daily Camera, as a child. The paper came to our doorstep every morning in the 1970s and 1980s, my growing-up years.

We—usually my brother and I, who were first up—brought the *Camera* into our house and unfolded it on our tables, couches, or on the floor in front of the heating vent on cold mountain mornings.

Aside from Garfield and Opus, I didn't see in it a reality that reflected life as I experienced it.

There was a lot of American football, even on the front page, and a lot of chatter about city council and criminal acts (none of which related to me). And, because I lived in a mountain town, there was a lot in the newspaper's pages about skiing—ski area openings and closings, highway traffic on the way to skiing, snow forecasts, ski clothing, ski trends.

But I did not ski. I still do not ski!

And while in the *Boulder Daily Camera* of yesteryear there was a good deal of coverage of schools (school politics, meetings, agendas, budgets), what was in the paper wasn't about what life was actually like in school (the activities, the programs, the people)—the texture of life as I knew it.

From the very beginning of my interactions with them, newspapers—and the news in them—did not reflect my reality. The notes I passed to friends did. The little mimeographed paper we created in fifth grade did (somewhat); the journal I wrote did (more so).

Perhaps it was audacious as a child to expect to see myself in those pages, but I did. My brothers saw themselves more: they were football fans. They experienced politics as more procedural and less relational than I did. I knew in a very intuitive way that the newspaper didn't reflect everyone's reality. I now know it reflected a slice of reality, typically—in my hometown certainly—a White, male, affluent reality.

In my adult life, as a reporter in the island city of Alameda, a community of about 75,000 in California's San Francisco Bay Area, I was deeply aware that my ideas about things—my support of the public schools, for example—informed my reporting.

> From the very beginning of my interactions with them, newspapers— and the news in them—did not reflect my reality.

My belief in the fundamental usefulness and importance of functional governments also informed my reporting.

My belief that a functional democracy relies on an informed, participatory citizenry informed my reporting.

My belief that I could support people in my town by parsing, investigating, articulating, and confirming information for them informed my reporting.

My belief, not fully articulated to myself at that time, that connection and relationship are the starting place for good, useful journalism informed my reporting.

That was my work.

I knew each time I made a choice—what story to cover (or not), whom to interview (or not), what data to include (or not), what questions to ask (or not), what quotes to use (or not)—those choices were informed by my definitions of importance and relevance, meaning and value, by who I was and where I came from.

My bias against American football came through when I chose not to write a story that a neighbor and football coach asked me to write about the formation of a new youth football league. (Because concussions.) My bias against the Boy Scouts came through when I wrote a long piece about a young man who had fulfilled all the requirements to be an Eagle Scout but then was denied his medal because he was openly gay.

Because of my awareness of some of my biases, I often felt like somewhat of a fraud, not a "real" journalist. I didn't carry myself with the same separateness and assurance that many of my peers seemed to.

It got a little better (meaning I felt like less of a fraud) when I became, in addition to a reporter, a blogger and columnist. In those roles, I was transparent about my opinions. In those contexts, I could write more honestly, more truthfully. I could say, "This is my view: this is why I think this policy or tax or program is good (or bad) for our community."

But I was also perplexed by this tension: the idea that I could write a story for the paper in the features or news section, ostensibly with no opinion, but then write a column with an explicit point of view. Both creations are products of the same me. And, yes, the style is different, but in either sort of writing, there are micro- and macro-choices being made at each and every juncture. How can we even dare suggest that there is no opinion in traditional or straight reporting?

The newest round of racial reckoning we are part of now in the United States is allowing for more consideration of the ways journalists' choices shape reporting. What has been left out of coverage? What is included? How much coverage is there about redlining and homeowner associations, school suspension and expulsion rates, access to fresh and healthy food by neighborhood, or emergency room treatment based on familial background? Do we see images and stories about successful Black people, for example? Whose reality does coverage reflect?

We have the same lapses in coverage, of course, with respect to gender and class, geography, and ideology. Who is featured and profiled? Who is quoted? (All studies show a relative absence of voices of color, of women, of the less affluent, of those who challenge accepted orthodoxies.)

Knowing the complexity and imperfection of human perception and of our society, what can journalists do? What can *I* do to support and create an informed public, an educated public, a public whose members need to be able to engage with one another about the issues that matter in a democracy?

After many years as a local reporter, columnist, and blogger for the *Alameda Journal*, I had the luck in 2010 to launch an all-digital local news site for Patch, an AOL-funded network of news sites.

The *Alameda Patch* I edited was built on a dynamic platform with room for people to post notices and blogs as well as comments and questions, and it came of age at a time when major social channels, Twitter and Facebook, were becoming integral parts of the news-gathering and news-sharing landscape. Patch was at the forefront of a new version of connection to community in a changing news landscape.

Patch management in New York City invited the editors of local sites (there were 900-plus across the country) to be open and forthright, to explain who we were and where we came from. I interpreted this as an invitation to dispense with false separateness, to dispense with the facade that reporters don't have views and ideas like everyone else. Patch's ethos, I believe, is the backbone of news done right and one that sat well with me. I could come clean with who I was and what I thought, and do my job as a reporter and editor. I could serve community and serve democracy.

The Wayback Machine Internet Archive yields my description of myself as it was posted on *Alameda Patch* for the years 2010 to 2013.[1]

About Eve

An Alameda resident since 2000, I have been writing about local politics and people since 2005. As editor of *Alameda Patch*, I enjoy bringing community news to island residents every day.

I earned a master's in journalism from Northwestern and a bachelor's degree from Cornell University. I live on Versailles Avenue with my two children and kind-hearted husband.

My beliefs: As a journalist, I honor and respect Patch's notion of quality news gathering: "At Patch, we promise always to report the facts as objectively as possible and otherwise adhere to the principles of good journalism. However, we also acknowledge that true impartiality is impossible because human beings have beliefs." Everyone comes with biases, perspectives, and viewpoints, but as journalists we strive to do our very best to report the facts and tell stories as objectively as possible.

My politics: Many may consider me to be liberal, but I'm conservative at heart: my interests and activities revolve around caring for family, community, and our planet's natural resources. One of my elemental beliefs is that the more we safeguard those among us who cannot care for themselves, the better off we all are.

My religion: I am culturally Jewish, but I am not religious. I admire and respect those who implement the truths held in common by all faiths—concern for the weak, the old, the poor, the needy; generosity; kindness; respect for living beings.

My aim as a journalist is to get the facts right and also to uncover the core issues behind the facts. And this effort, like life, is always a work in progress. We become better reporters/writers/thinkers when we acknowledge that we do not always have all the answers.

In terms of community involvement, I have been active in the public school system, volunteering in many ways, and I have served on my children's school's site council as well as on the board of the Alameda Education Foundation. My husband, an attorney, served until this spring on the City of Alameda's Social Service Human Relations Board and has also been active with the Community Alliance Resource for Education (CARE). He currently serves on the board of the nonprofit Alternatives In Action.

I believe, like Patch, in local news that enlightens the community by inviting civil dialogue and helping us to better understand each other.

Alameda Hot Button Issues

Schools: I believe that our nation has been built on quality public schools and we are all made better if we fund them well. Although I believe that under the constraints of Proposition 13 no school parcel tax can be fair, I have supported all the recent school taxes in Alameda.

Development: I support intelligent and sensible development.

Change: Not all that is new is better, but it should be.

Community Identity: We are made stronger when we promote the general welfare.

Role of Government: I don't believe that there is a giant conspiracy, that all who do public service are evil, or that someone is always out to get us, but I do believe that institutions are created by humans, some wise, some generous, some highly ethical, others selfish and dishonest, and that all of us humans are, of course, wildly imperfect.

Alameda Point: Truthfully? If I were the boss of all things, and money were no object, I would clean it all up to the highest possible standard, create acres of parklands with bay front trails. I would also create a promenade, with restaurants and stores and apartments along the bay with a view of it and San Francisco. I'd like a carousel along the water with open space for people to gather and enjoy the bay views and breezes. I would rehab some of the old buildings. I like the idea of senior living communities and also of preserving the businesses and communities that are already established on The Point. But I am not queen and Alameda, though a lovely city, is not a utopia. And that is where, it seems, the rancor begins.

I wrote that I cared about schools and community. I wrote that I supported intentional development as well as investment in local infrastructure, buildings, and humans alike. Instead of pretending I didn't have views, I was transparent about them. It felt like renewal.

I learned over time that in addition to helping me feel good, my openness engendered trust. And I learned that when I proved myself reasonable and responsive and respectful, it engendered respect. There is so much talk about lack of trust in journalism, but I believe that good old-fashioned relationship building is one path out.

I learned that I could be me, openly, without artifice. I could be me without pretending I was infallible or all-knowing, and do my job to inform and serve the community. It is not simply that I *could* do it, and not simply that I was better off for it, but also that my community, the people, with whom I was sharing information, were better off for it. With trust and connection, I could be a resource, clarify readers' understandings and misunderstandings, and provide useful and relevant knowledge. This created a strong, valuable, feedback loop. Over and over in those years, in online formats and in person, people would ask me questions or make comments. I could help clarify: *Actually, that is not what that ordinance does; it . . . Actually, she voted for that resolution last week, not against it. Actually, the Piedmont Soccer Club is using 80 percent of Alameda fields every weekend.*

My role as community researcher and explainer flourished. Because in addition to cultivating relationships, I have a discipline: I can be accurate with numbers, facts, and details. I can check and double-check. I can pay attention, assimilate, assess, articulate, query, synthesize, explain.

My allegiance is toward truth and accuracy, both about who I am and what I believe as a person AND about what information I gather and share with others. These things are not oppositional. My journalism is better for both of them.

If It's Broke, Try to Fix It

I have many obsessions. A cluster of them center on things we do as humans that don't make sense. Consider lawns. Lawns are sensible in places where it rains year-round, but in coastal California where it doesn't rain for nine or ten months a year? Are lawns sensible in *any* place where the water to maintain grass lawns is processed, pumped, purified, and piped? What a colossal waste of energy and resources.

We have grown our lawns mindlessly, perhaps because it is what is "normal"; perhaps because that is what the neighbors are doing; perhaps because that is what our parents did.

As a gardener who planted through several decades of California droughts, I learned to grow plants that thrive in the coastal climate: thymes, sages, tea trees, Santa Barbara daisies.

My discomfort with the dominant practices of traditional journalism was heightened in the run-up to the 2016 election as I observed the ugliness and dehumanization of our public spaces and the accelerated fracturing of our information infrastructure. That which had been simmering began to boil—the constriction of trusted voices and publications, the uptick in nefarious actors working diligently to divide and polarize us—all of which strain our democracy. Our nation's journalism practices and our journalistic institutions were doing what we had always done, even as the landscape was changing.

I started to think more deeply about what I might do if I were practicing my journalism in a way that made as much sense as possible in response to the moment. What could I do in response to these pressures and concerns amid a rapidly changing information ecosystem? I mulled it over. What could I grow?

As a local news reporter and editor, I had already taken many turns at supporting the public square—moderating comments and conversations online and in person, editing columns and letters to the editor, advising on blog posts and community announcements. I wondered how I might use these moderating/mediating skills and my more traditional journalistic tool kit—vetting, researching, assessing, and sharing information—to more directly support conversations across the ever-growing divides in our public space? How could I be part of a repair?

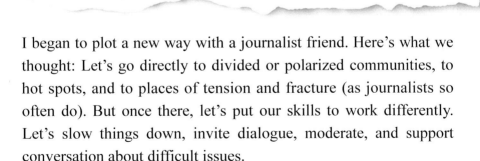

Instead of highlighting the most extreme positions, let's invite nuance, decency, respect, and actual conversation.

I began to plot a new way with a journalist friend. Here's what we thought: Let's go directly to divided or polarized communities, to hot spots, and to places of tension and fracture (as journalists so often do). But once there, let's put our skills to work differently. Let's slow things down, invite dialogue, moderate, and support conversation about difficult issues.

Instead of highlighting the most extreme positions, let's invite nuance, decency, respect, and actual conversation. Then let's give people the information that they need to talk about issues. Let's invite regular people to shed the ugliness of current discourse and ask them to join in a respectful dialogue about issues they care passionately about. Let's invite them in as whole people, individuals with complicated stories and views.

So was born Dialogue Journalism, a seven-step process for convening and hosting journalism-supported conversations across social and political fault lines. We worked in partnership with established newsrooms to identify a polarizing issue relevant to that publication's audience. They suggested issues such as educational policy, farming practices, immigration. And then we brought people together, often online, for monthlong engagements.

When people signed up, they were asked for basic demographic details so we could create a group that represented the community. We also asked for topic-specific information so we could represent a spectrum of beliefs and ideas. We then asked them four core questions. The first two invited curiosity, connection, and relationship.

1. What do you want to know about the other side?
2. What do you want them to know about you?

And then we asked:

3. What do you think about them?
4. What do you think they think about you?

These last two questions surfaced people's reflexive, negative stereotypes about the other "side." When we shared the answers back to the participants anonymously, people were nearly universally able to see the stereotypes cast in relief, to see that they said some pretty nasty things about a large group of "others." They were able to recognize that "certainly not *everyone* who thinks differently from me is so awful." Once articulated, we could look these ugly stereotypes in the eye so people could move forward into real dialogue.

As we moderated our conversations, we invited people to shake off the uncivil norms. We asked them to slow down, to be their best selves. We asked people to ask genuine questions, to assume good intentions of the other side, to share their personal experiences. We found, over a dozen or so projects over three years, that when we showed up real and authentic, transparent about who we were (people with values, views, and ideas) and clear about what our goals were (to support constructive, informed dialogue because democracy requires it), people would do their very best to engage constructively.

As I had learned earlier in my career, when I tell my story truthfully, without pretending, it engenders trust. As a journalist-moderator, I didn't pretend that I am not exactly what I am: an educated, White, Jewish, female, and the product of elite universities and coastal communities (or progressive college towns) in the United States. I have strong political opinions, and I was transparent about them as well. Despite this (or because of it), I could be a respectful, effective moderator, a useful provider of information.

In our conversations, instead of reporting in a narrative form, we reported with what we call FactStacks. These issue-focused briefs are like explainers, and we created them in direct response to what people were discussing so that they could have accurate facts to support their discussions. While people disagree about the meaning of facts and how they ought to inform policy, once they trusted us, they could believe our reporting—which is of significant value in this era. In FactStacks we showed our work and explained our choices. We explained where we found information and why we chose to include it. Our transparency and responsiveness modeled behavior for the conversation participants.

We know from other parts of our lives that people don't extend trust because they are told to; we know that trust is earned over time. Yet, as journalists, we sometimes default to demanding that readers or listeners "trust science" or "trust me, I'm a journalist" or at our worst, with a foot stamp, "trust me because I am right!" None of this helps make matters better.

We also know from a lifetime of experience (if not from social science research), that when you call people names (racist, snowflake, backward, socialist, sexist, weird, stupid), it exacerbates tensions and reduces the possibility of understanding. We know, too, that if we as convenors show up as honest and forthright, people respond to that.

Often people ask me whether these conversation experiences, moderated by journalists, are "real" journalism. Usually I say something like this: if our role is to communicate and if our writing and videos, and tweets and columns are not being trusted, read, or respected, then our communication is not working and we need to do something different. We need to consider, what *will* grow?

Spaceship Media was launched by considering how we might interrupt cycles of mistrust and distrust in journalists, how we might interrupt the dehumanization and nastiness in our public spaces, and how we might build community across disagreement.

There are many forces—economic, technological, sociological, psychological, and historical—working against journalists' ability to fulfill our best, most altruistic aims, but part of our work must be to consider, reflect, challenge, and interrogate our practices. We must be as thoughtful and agile as we can be. If what we're doing isn't working, if people don't trust us, if civil dialogue is contracting, how can we adapt our practices to better serve our highest calling, supporting our democracy? Spaceship Media's Dialogue Journalism is one effort to adapt to the reality of today's civic information landscape.

My allegiance is toward truth and accuracy, both about who I am and what I believe as a person AND about what information I gather and share with others. These things are not oppositional. My journalism is better for both of them.

Look In to Look Out

Journalists are very often my favorite people. Most of my best friends are journalists, and I know that it takes a lot of guts to make a story from bits and pieces of this and that, from interviews and documents, to do this again and again under pressure from deadlines, knowing your results will be shared for many to see, critique, challenge, judge.

These acts of creative production take confidence and certainty, and while the work is very often driven by curiosity and a desire to serve, the practice does not necessarily invite certain kinds of self-reflection and openness.

When we launched Spaceship, we knew the problems in our communities were not just about the mistrust of each side for the other, but also about the mistrust of journalists. Dialogue Journalism is meant to create a triangle of trust between journalists and the divided communities they serve. Key to this effort is transparency, asking ourselves as journalists to be open about who we are, what we think and believe, and what we are doing—as we invite others, the journalists and community members we work with, to do the same.

The more you understand about who you are and where you come from, and the more open you are about it, the better you can serve other people. The more you recognize and acknowledge the particularities of your own experiences and identity, the less time you need to spend contorting yourself to match the claim we are so often hampered by: that journalists can be neutral or invisible arbiters of information. Someone is always telling the story.

Dialogue Journalism is meant to create a triangle of trust between journalists and the divided communities they serve.

Creating and hosting Dialogue Journalism conversations were my efforts to reconceptualize the Fourth Estate, to respond to the reality of the existing information ecosystem. I did this explicitly, directly, intentionally, and collaboratively, and it has been tremendously gratifying to help create experiences for people in which they start out with disdain, mistrust, and anger but end up with the ability to talk with one another.

I believe that the more openly you can look with clear eyes at those with whom you engage and the more you can look with clear eyes at yourself—your history, values, ideas, experiences, prejudices, biases, and habits of practice—the richer your work will be and the more likely you will be to earn trust, build community, and support a broader, more dynamic, more inclusive society with your journalism.

Given what we know about how humans think and act, so much of how journalists are responding to this crisis of dehumanization in the information ecosystem doesn't make sense. In an era of mistrust and skepticism, with people on heightened alert for being manipulated and played, the way out for journalists is to be as forthright and transparent as possible. Carry your pursuit of truth and accuracy into an effort to understand where you, with your perspectives and biases, come from. Deep authenticity is the way out of what feels like an impossible situation for our news and information systems. These are rough times. We must lead with bold, brave, and supple toughness, and embrace reality in all its complexity, external and internal.

Deepening our focus and learning to be more intentional about who we are and where we come from must be the new underpinning of our journalistic practices, our dialogic practices, and our work as part of the community that is our democracy.

My allegiance is toward truth and accuracy, both about who I am and what I believe as a person AND about what information I gather and share with others. These things are not oppositional. My journalism is better for both of them.

A Framework for Building Trust with Communities

by David Plazas

M cMinnville, Tennessee, sits 80 miles east of popular sunbelt city, Nashville, also known as Music City, the "it" city, and the Athens of the South.

Nashville is the city I have lived in for eight years. When the *Tennessean* news publication hired me to lead its opinion section, I chose to move to one of its densest, most urban areas because it felt like home to this Chicago native.

McMinnville, on the other hand, is a bucolic, quaint small town. Its downtown is perfect for a postcard or the setting for a Hallmark Channel movie.

Here are a couple of more relevant comparisons.

Population

Nashville's population in 2020 was about 715,884 residents, growing 14 percent over the last decade.[1] McMinnville's population is just shy of 14,000—about 2 percent higher than it was in 2010.[2] That means the town grew by fewer than 200 people.

Presidential Politics

As for voting, in the 2016 presidential election, 60 percent of Nashville-Davidson County voters chose Hillary Clinton while 70 percent of Warren County residents picked Donald Trump.[3] McMinnville is the seat of Warren County. In 2020, nearly 65 percent of Nashville voters selected Joe Biden and nearly 74 percent of Warren voters opted for Trump.[4]

These two communities are emblematic of the nation's growing urban-rural divide and the stark polarization that is afflicting the United States today.

> My boss challenged me to start a campaign revolving around civil discourse.

For centuries, the American two-party system has created conditions for people to view the world, politics, and policy in radically different ways. In recent years, however, with the advent of social media, issues such as the Affordable Care Act, abortion, gun rights, COVID-19, the Capitol insurrection, critical race theory, and LGBTQ+ rights have worsened these divides and threaten to destroy our pluralistic democratic society.

On April 26, 2018, I made my way to McMinnville for the first time, taking a charming route to a place where I knew the people would be courteous but dubious of me because of my line of work. Over the last several decades, Gallup has documented the drop in trust Americans have in institutions.[5] The latest poll showed only 21 percent of Americans trusted newspapers.

I was heading to McMinnville because the Rotary Club had invited me to talk about a new initiative, called Civility Tennessee, that the *Tennessean* had started under my leadership.[6]

As a news organization and as journalists, we were very concerned with the growing polarization and animus since the 2016 election. People ended friendships, screamed at each other on social media, and demonized those who did not go along with their views.

I was present at the state's General Assembly House of Representatives chambers in December 2016 when Tennessee electors affirmed then President-Elect Donald Trump's victory in the state.[7] The chair, in a stern voice, said they were fulfilling the "will of the people." A protestor in the gallery screamed: "It's *not* the will of the people." The two Americas that commentators often talk about starkly revealed themselves that day. Nearly a year later, my boss challenged me to start a campaign revolving around civil discourse.

I was finishing up a very successful yearlong series examining affordable housing in Nashville, which involved long-form columns, three community forums, and a documentary.[8] I started research for this effort a year before we published a single word and learned about the importance of the subject to citizens deeply concerned about Nashville's cost of living. I rode the bus weekly and listened to riders' conversations; I took frequent ride-shares on the weekends and chatted with multiple drivers. Their concerns centered around the city's rising cost of living and housing costs. Nashville was booming, but these people were being left behind.

I enjoyed going in-depth on meaty topics that were tangible. Rising housing costs and growing income inequality were facts and could be measured. Civil discourse? That was far more subjective and I had major misgivings. We were living through an era when former friends were unfriending, trolling, and insulting each other because of differences in their politics. Trying to create bridges in the midst of polarity felt daunting. But I like a challenge, and I felt very disconcerted by the threat polarization posed to democracy.

So, Civility Tennessee was born.[9]

What Is Civility Tennessee?

The drive to McMinnville is picturesque. Once one gets to the downtown, you see several churches lining the main strip, charming houses, and a lot of greenery. The Rotary Club created a brochure announcing my visit with the headline, "Restoring Civility in Public Discourse." The subheadline read: "Media Giant Gannett Launches Civility Tennessee."

I felt a lot of pressure to deliver. The campaign was barely four months old, and my staff and I were still trying to figure things out.

Up to that point, we had created a strategy with four pillars:

- To encourage conversations that are civil and respectful, even if they are hard

- To enhance civic participation in important conversations ranging from transit to local elections to the gubernatorial and senatorial races

- To help promote voter registration efforts

- To increase news literacy and enhance trust of the *Tennessean* and sister publications

Our inaugural event featured conservative author and lobbyist Jim Brown who wrote *Ending Our Uncivil War*.[10] Vanderbilt University hosted the evening and its former chancellor, Nicholas Zeppos, introduced the program, which gave our effort a boost.

We had two well-viewed virtual events on Facebook Live with experts I interviewed to discuss how to engage others on difficult topics such as racism[11] and gun violence.[12]

And we had just hosted a debate at the Nashville Public Library on a controversial multibillion-dollar transit plan pushed by the city.[13] But we had never taken the show outside of Nashville to—dare I say it—a red county.

A Blue Dot in a Red State

Metro Nashville (the city and county are consolidated) is exceptionally blue in its politics, and it is 1 of only 3 in 95 counties in Tennessee where most voters picked the Democratic presidential candidate.

Tennessee is an overwhelmingly red state. The Tennessee General Assembly had been run by Democrats for more than a century until 2010 when the tide changed. Today, Republicans have supermajorities in the state House and Senate.

It used to be the pendulum would swing on gubernatorial politics. Since 1970, Tennessee voters had alternated between Republican and Democratic governors. That changed in 2018, when air conditioning company CEO Bill Lee, a Republican, succeeded fellow Republican Bill Haslam as governor.[14] Lee beat his Democratic opponent by more than 20 percentage points.

"Why Should I Trust You?"

As I walked into the Rotary Club in rural McMinnville at a local church in 2018, my nerves settled a bit. The McMinnville Rotarians were a friendly bunch. They shared their fried chicken, greens, and cherry pie with me. The leaders conducted their traditional introductory rituals and offered announcements before it was my turn to speak.

I was given 20 minutes, and I spoke to the audience for just half of that. I planned to listen and respond to questions for the second half. My speech focused on what Civility Tennessee is, why we were doing it, and a description of our recent events.

When the Q&A started, a gentleman raised his hand, stood up, cleared his throat, and asked boldly, "Why should I trust you?"

Those words echoed in my head.

"Why should I trust you?"

He explained that he was not out to accuse me personally, but he believed that journalists had failed at their jobs by creating the impression that Hillary Clinton's victory was inevitable and by taking an adversarial stance against Donald Trump. He also alluded to the impression rural communities have that "media elites" looked down upon people like him, and he resented it.

Two years before, I had been dumbstruck that more than 60 percent of my fellow state residents favored Trump. That moment at the 2018 Rotary Club meeting was the start of a series of "aha" moments for me.

I realized that Civility Tennessee was far more important and essential than I had recognized and that I had to shed my impostor syndrome feelings and assume the role with full confidence. Even though my engagement work had focused on bringing communities together on tangible topics, as an editorial writer, I had often taken adversarial stances against government officials over the years. This new initiative required me to go from occasional pugilist to nearly full-time conciliator.

There is a photo of me from 2019 when I spoke to Minneapolis business leaders about Civility Tennessee. I am standing in front of a screen giving a slide presentation and the slide that appears in that moment says:

"Questions journalists need to be able to answer: Why should we trust you?"

I keep that photo on my desk. It is a reminder that this is a question we in the press need to answer every single day.

A study by the Pew Research Center shows that only a fifth of Americans have ever met or spoken to a journalist.[15] In 2021, the American Press Institute (API) found in its research that most Americans don't cherish the same values journalists do.[16] The research showed that while journalists hold certain values dear—factualism, giving voice, social criticism, oversight, and transparency—it would behoove them to understand people's perceptions of news through the lens of their own moral values. The respondents tended to value factualism, but many also perceived journalists to have a slant on news coverage, which created trust issues.

This helps explain why people's impressions of the press tend to be negative—that we look down on them, that we publish only news that makes subjects and the world look worse than they are, that we are willing to sacrifice ethics for a good story that will draw a bunch of clicks. This explains the distrust and mistrust that cause some Americans to turn their backs on the press and embrace misinformation and disinformation, sometimes to the detriment of their lives, as we have seen with COVID-19.

I am grateful to the McMinnville Rotarian because he allowed me to answer his question. I explained the aspirations of the campaign, I acknowledged our errors, and I did my best to send a hopeful message. I did my best to be humble instead of combative.

He thanked me politely and sat down.

Why Trust Matters

Throughout the Civility Tennessee campaign, which is now in its sixth year, my staff and I have worked with partners to help us learn, strategize, and pivot when necessary.

The Trusting News organization, a project of the Donald W. Reynolds Journalism Institute (RJI) and the American Press Institute (API), works on helping news organizations earn trust from community members.[17] This is a valuable asset that helped us focus on explaining to the public how and why we make our decisions. It sounds simple, but we rarely do it and then wonder why a reader or viewer does not understand why we published a particular story or viewpoint. Trusting News reminded us that labels (i.e., "opinion" for commentary to distinguish from news) and explanations by editors about our process matter greatly.

We partnered with volunteer organizations such as the citizen-run nonprofit Braver Angels (formerly known as Better Angels) to learn listening techniques that help with building personal relationships with ideologically diverse groups of people before jumping into a political discussion.[18]

In addition to working with Vanderbilt University and the Nashville library system, we also developed programming with other universities, including Belmont, Cumberland, Memphis, and Lipscomb, where we held our best-attended event on voting in the state.[19] In the recent past, Tennessee ranked 50th in voter turnout, and we thought it was important to understand why and how to move the needle.

The reasons for the low turnout included changes in law (stemming from Supreme Court decisions on voting rights) that allowed states to create stricter barriers to voting. After the 2013 Supreme Court decision in *Shelby v. Holder*, Tennessee changed laws to require a strict identification card requirement. However, unlike other states, Tennessee did not alter its voting laws after the 2020 election. After all, Trump handily won the state.

Another activity was a book club around historian Jon Meacham's *The Soul of America* that allowed for intimate interactions among citizens.[20] We again partnered with the Nashville Public Library and offered 50 seats for a book club discussion, which included time for citizens to talk about the book in a small setting and then share their insights with the larger group. Literacy and examining history critically are essential for a healthy civil society.

We also refined our definition of civility.

In the summer of 2018, there was a lot of pushback on the term *civility* after former White House Press Secretary Sarah Huckabee Sanders was kicked out of a Virginia restaurant. She and other peers urged citizens to be civil. The criticism against her was that she was advocating for policies and making statements that several citizens found uncivil and, in some cases, exaggerated or dishonest.

We had already heard criticism of our campaign name because some people, such as progressives, thought civility was impossible in the Trump age. Others, including people in marginalized and underrepresented communities of color, had seen the word used as a cudgel against them when they advocated for equal rights.

I wrote a column headlined "On Civility: Don't Be Nice, Be a Good Citizen," in which I argued that we needed to shed the modern interpretation of the word that equates civility with politeness, courtesy, and acquiescence.[21]

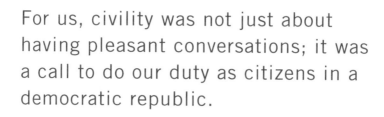

For us, civility was not just about having pleasant conversations; it was a call to do our duty as citizens in a democratic republic.

The root of *civility* is the Latin *civitas*, which means: "1) the body of citizens who constitute a state, especially a city-state, commonwealth, or the like; and 2) citizenship, especially as imparting shared responsibility, a common purpose, and sense of community," according to Dictionary.com.

For us, civility was not just about having pleasant conversations; it was a call to do our duty as citizens in a democratic republic. This means working together, despite our differences, to create a healthy and equitable society beneficial to citizens enjoying life, liberty, and the pursuit of happiness. We wanted to support the citizens of Tennessee in doing this work.

There is a school of thought that we should drop efforts to build, preserve, or reestablish trust, which is critical to our work to build bridges and understanding. I understand. It is a lot of work—any relationship is. And sometimes it doesn't work. But relationships of trust yield great benefits: among them, that people will listen. They don't have to agree, but sometimes they may be persuaded and other times they help change our minds, too.

Without trust, the *Tennessean* might have suffered a devastating blow.

The Islamophobic Ad Incident

In June 2020, the *Tennessean* print newspaper published two full-page ads by a zealous, Islamophobic religious sect that sought to discredit Islam.[22] As sales and news operate separately, our journalists had no warning.

The first ad, published on a Wednesday, was cryptic. The second one, which ran on the following Sunday, claimed that someone named "Islam" was going to detonate a nuclear device at Nashville's city hall.

The claims were nonsensical, and it is not completely clear to me why this group would go to so much trouble and pay so much money, except to stoke fear and turn people against Muslim citizens. It was embarrassing, and dangerous, especially to the community of Muslims in Tennessee who had struggled with bigotry and hateful rhetoric over the years.

The criticism of the *Tennessean* on social media was brutal and searing.

The *Tennessean*'s editorial board, on which I serve, quickly began reaching out to leaders in the Muslim community with whom we had developed strong relationships over the years. We had attended events at local mosques. We had hosted tables at the annual Community *Iftar* to celebrate Ramadan and encouraged interfaith conversations. The multifaceted—and less stereotyped—representations of Muslims had grown in our news and opinion pages.

Without that history, starting from square one to recover from this scandal would likely have been impossible.

The sales side terminated the manager responsible for approving the ad and agreed to offer print and digital space for efforts to bridge gaps and educate Americans about their Muslim neighbors. The editorial board convened a meeting via Zoom the following day, and over the next several days we developed and executed a plan to explain to the public what happened. We scheduled deep training for our staff, which included mandatory presentations and Q&As with A Million Conversations, the American Muslim Advisory Council, and Jonathan Metzl, author of *Dying of Whiteness*. We also used our print and digital platforms to elevate and amplify the voices of Muslim leaders on the editorial side (news and opinion).[23]

By the end of the year, Samar Ali, an influential leader who is Muslim, agreed to participate on a panel on reconciliation, hosted by our parent company Gannett's interfaith employee resource group. This was a conversation I moderated with five diverse speakers, including Ali and Keith Allred, executive director of the National Institute for Civil Discourse. Our panelists spoke and answered our employees' questions about the importance of reconciliation in the COVID-19 era and in the wake of a contentious and divisive presidential election.

Today, Ali cochairs Vanderbilt University's Project on Unity and American Democracy. Her friendship and trust was critical to helping us get through this crisis. As a news organization, we have a responsibility to learn from this incident, make things right, and do better. It was important to use this approach in order to have deep connections to communities of diverse ideologies, including conservative residents who felt treated unfairly by traditional media organizations.

One major step we took was hiring Cameron Smith as a new columnist in June 2021.[24] He is a former political attorney who worked in national Republican politics and once served former US Senator Jeff Sessions. While our opinion and engagement team has made inroads to increase the publication of conservative voices in the *Tennessean*, the perception lingers that conservatives are not welcome because of the *Tennessean*'s 100-plus-year history of aligning editorially with the Democratic Party. (Democrats were endorsed for president of the United States from 1908 to 2008.) Creating spaces for people of diverse ideological backgrounds is important to the civility work.

Social Media Etiquette

Social media poses a challenge and an opportunity when it comes to building trust. When I decided to get on Twitter in 2008, I had no idea how to use it. On September 26, 2008, I tweeted for the first time, "I am on a call about leveraging our social networking strategy."[25] I tweeted four times that year. Some 13 years later, I have tweeted thousands of times, but a platform that was supposed to be about sharing activities and connecting with others has become a space for trolling, doxing, feuding, and obscuring the facts.

I still use Twitter, but I am a lot more cautious than I used to be, and I do not engage in back-and-forth pointless arguments. I found that feuding became a narcissistic pursuit that distracted from our public service mission.

The ephemeral nature of Twitter is that the issue will often go away. A careless and angry tweet, however, may follow someone in life and work for a long time. As a preacher's kid, I grew up with the adage in the Letter of James to be quick to listen, slow to speak, and slow to anger. This mantra was essential for my mental health and our reputations. We journalists should be leery of letting reckless tweeting or posting distract from our reporting, writing, and broadcasting. Such recklessness has the potential to hurt our organizations' credibility and discredit us with sources and as professionals. I often tell colleagues that if a tweet enrages them, it's best to take a break from the mobile device and take a walk or do some other such grounding activity. There is value in social media. However, one must be mindful of messaging. One must be attentive to those who truly want to connect and disengage from those who want to harm you. This is essential in practicing journalism that is about engaging communities and building trust.

Civility Tennessee became for me a way to practice civil discourse on an online platform. Some of the lessons in real life were invaluable for the virtual world we have found ourselves in throughout the COVID-19 pandemic.

When I delivered a speech for TEDx Nashville in September 2020 about the issue of public disagreement and "adult" conversations, I outlined some tips:[26]

> Stop feuding.
> Don't respond hastily.
> Learn to disengage.
> In person is best.

These are easier said than done, but they are essential to preserving one's wits, growing community, and building trust.

Finding Community during a Pandemic

When community members can convene in person, over coffee or over a meal, for example, there is a greater chance to build and develop a relationship. When COVID-19 emerged in March 2020, city and countywide shutdowns made many of these types of interaction a thing of the past.

At the *Tennessean*, we saw it also as an opportunity. It gave us a chance to create a new experience that connected the community with diverse groups of leaders who could help citizens understand what was happening in the pandemic and provide them some hope.

The *Tennessee Voices* video podcast, which I host, debuted on March 24, 2020.[27] The 20-minute show offers a conversation with people of varied backgrounds and political affiliations working on interesting projects that elevate the common good or influence public opinion. Nonprofit leaders fighting for reproductive rights have been featured as have conservative Republican US senators. By the end of December 2022, *Tennessee Voices* had produced 329 episodes, with more to come.

In addition, our staff struggled with how the pandemic conditions might affect our efforts to improve our engagement with underrepresented communities. We were working with the API to help us design experiments to build trust and grow our audience. In the spring of 2021, we decided to focus on the African American community, which represented more than a quarter of Nashville's population.

What we wanted to do was to shift our perspective from telling stories *about* members of the Black community to telling stories *for* and *with* them. We used tools API taught us to create a strategy and tactics, compare our assumptions with facts, and quickly design experiments to better serve the community. The murder of George Floyd in Minneapolis on Memorial Day 2020 and the subsequent protests and conversations on racial reckoning accelerated our urgency to act.

> What we wanted to do was to shift our perspective from telling stories *about* members of the Black community to telling stories *for* and *with* them.

By the end of 2020, we had started a *Black Tennessee Voices* newsletter[28] and a *Black Tennessee Voices* Facebook group,[29] both curated by my engagement team member, the columnist LeBron Hill. *Editor & Publisher* featured *Black Tennessee Voices* in its November 2021 magazine.[30]

The effort has yielded growth—a higher-than-average newsletter open rate, active participation in the Facebook group, and a doubling of the number of guest essays submitted by Black writers. These essays have run the gamut from personal stories of being harmed by racism to advocating policy positions in education, health care, and criminal justice reform.

The weekly newsletter allowed for a trusted voice from the community to weave together some of the most compelling columns and stories about the Black experience, from the pain of police brutality to the celebration of milestones. The intent was to grow an audience that is underrepresented in coverage and readership and also to show that we were willing to invest in our newsroom by hiring more journalists of color.

A *Black Voices* special section in June sent a powerful message to the community as a whole.[31] It focused on Black citizens' candid reflections on experiencing and combating racism. The section elicited great empathy and community support. There were occasional racist missives complaining about seeing too many Black people represented, but we didn't get many of them.

We found, too, that the *Tennessee Voices* episodes with Black guests showed a higher rate of viewership and engagement by the general public than episodes with White guests.

The *Tennessean* and the USA TODAY Network's commitment to telling stories for the Black community extended to major critically acclaimed projects including Hallowed Sound,[32] about Black influence in music, including country music; and Confederate Reckoning,[33] an examination of Confederate symbols, which won the Robert F. Kennedy Award in June 2021.[34] The award's judges made special note of the video panel conducted by the network with the founders of the Fuller Story, a campaign in Franklin, Tennessee, to add context around a Confederate monument and also tell the stories of Black residents throughout the city's history.

Based upon the success of *Black Tennessee Voices*, the *Tennessean* launched a *Latino Tennessee Voices* newsletter on September 15, 2021.[35]

Building Trust Takes a Team

The engagement work of the *Tennessean* has intentionally sought to bridge gaps; to develop, preserve, and rebuild relationships; and to make trust fundamental to these efforts.

In addition to our outward-facing efforts, the *Tennessean* and the USA TODAY Network have taken significant steps to enhance diversity in our newsrooms and to offer extensive training on topics such as investigative reporting and cultural competency.[36]

Convening internal conversations through our monthly Diversity and Inclusion Task Force meetings and at other regular staff meetings is important to helping communicate our values, efforts, and commitment to our newsroom. Those deeper relationships lead to greater understanding, a higher rate of news literacy, and a commitment to sustain democracy.

The work of building and keeping public trust is not the job of one individual alone. It takes a dedicated team that is willing to do the work to drive the momentum forward, manage crises effectively, and keep the focus on our public service mission. This is about meaningful and intentional public service for our fellow citizens in order to help preserve and strengthen our democratic republic. The question, "Why should I trust you?" should be top of mind daily to journalists, who must be responsive in order to be successful in their work.

For Democracy to Work, Journalism Needs an Ethic of Care

by Linda Miller

In April 2011, I attended a two-day gathering at the MIT Center for Civic Media to explore what's possible for communities and democracy when journalists and librarians work together.

At the time, I was the director of American Public Media's (APM's) Public Insight Network (PIN), a national initiative to help journalists do community engagement and diversify their sources. I was invited to Boston, in part, to talk about LibrariUS, an ongoing collaboration among PIN, the American Library Association, and the Public Library Association. We had created a web tool to collect stories—displayed on an interactive map and updated in real time—about the role of libraries in people's lives and in their communities. More than 700 libraries had embedded the LibrariUS widget on their home pages, prompting 3,000-plus patrons and library staff to share their insights and experiences, creating a dynamic picture of people bettering themselves and their communities.

My favorite LibrariUS story came from a librarian in Notus, Idaho, who wrote about the need to create spaces that connect people to each other, to their communities, and to credible, relevant, and actionable information:

We do not have a barber, beauty shop, or coffee shop where people can congregate. The bar is not an option for most, especially women. So women come in the library to get acquainted with their new village. Some connect with us through preschool story time weekly. Others wander in to check our book selection. I work very hard at connecting newcomers to an oldcomer (for lack of a better word); I will directly introduce them and mention something that might interest both. It usually works. I learned about four years ago, when we had an ongoing jigsaw puzzle on the table, it gave women a reason to linger. So I make sure one is always in progress. Two volunteers, both with much experience with alcoholics, abuse and depression, work on the puzzle and welcome new women to join them. Domestic violence is discussed, as are relationships with men and kids. Financial issues come up; at times the community has been able to pull together to provide the food, gas, or whatever else is needed (coat, washing machine).

As I recited her words that day in Boston, librarians around the room nodded in agreement, and one summed up the sentiment with a Theodore Roosevelt quote: "People don't care how much you know until they know how much you care."

More than a few journalists present were, well, puzzled.

It's OK for journalists to care about issues, stories, accuracy, seeking truth, and holding the powerful to account. But openly caring about people or communities? That interferes with news judgment, or so we are taught. The consequences are more severe if you are a Black, Indigenous, or other journalist whose right to exist is widely politicized and marginalized in and by the media.

As Pacinthe Mattar, a writer and producer in Toronto, put it: "Our professionalism is questioned when we report on the communities we're from, and the spectre of advocacy follows us in a way that it does not follow many of our White colleagues."[1] It can even get you banned from covering certain stories or fired.[2]

Yet, if journalists cannot advocate for their communities' well-being, what, exactly, is their purpose?

> We need journalism grounded in an ethic of care.

For democracy to work as it should, we need healthy communities, and healthy communities need civic infrastructure that supports and enables broad-based participation in governance, education, the economy, and civic life. We need resilient and diverse local media ecosystems with a mutual aid mindset that is rooted in listening, reciprocity, subsidiarity, and solidarity. We need journalists willing to challenge bias, change problematic narratives, and create social capital.

We need journalism grounded in an ethic of care.

That conference in Boston was a turning point for me, one of many that have helped me see not just how dehumanized, depersonalized, irrelevant, and uncaring journalism has become but all that we stand to lose if we don't fix it.

It would take 10 more years, many more collaborations, and a lot of listening and self-reflection before I could truly connect those dots and realize that for journalism to truly strengthen communities, we must also change who informs it, who forms it, and who benefits from it.

Defining Care

I became a journalist in the small towns of Wyoming, where newspapers were pieced together with hot wax and border tape and held together by trust, transparency, and a partnership with readers. My first job out of college in 1993 was as editor of the *Pinedale Roundup*, a weekly newspaper and the only news outlet in Sublette County which, at the time, consisted of 3.2 million acres of mostly public land, 5,000 people, and zero stoplights.

There was no curbside mail delivery; readers had to retrieve the paper from their post office boxes or buy it off the rack. The *Roundup* ran only locally reported news—no wire service stories—and on the day the paper was published, I would hang out at the local cafés and bars to hear readers complain about all the stories we missed and all the ads we didn't.

The *Roundup* may have been owned by the publisher of the *Jackson Hole Guide* 70 miles north, but it was a community asset. As editor and steward of that asset, I owed a duty of care to the communities it served, which in the minds of many, precluded running ads from competing businesses in other counties.

To be clear, there is no explicit duty of care in journalism ethics, only an admonition to "minimize harm."[3] The discomfort of advertisers is not the primary consideration. The Society of Professional Journalists Code of Ethics says journalists should "treat sources, subjects, colleagues and members of the public as human beings deserving of respect," and "balance the public's need for information against potential harm or discomfort."

One possible takeaway is that "care," as a journalistic ethic, is defined primarily as respect for others. But this limited interpretation discounts the many other aspects of ethical journalism that help define it as a care practice.

In a 2011 interview, psychologist and feminist scholar Carol Gilligan, for instance, defines the ethics of care within a democratic framework as

> a human ethic grounded in core democratic values: the importance of everyone having a voice, being listened to carefully and heard with respect. The premise of equal voice then allows conflicts to be addressed in relationships. Different voices then become integral to the vitality of a democratic society.[4]

It's not hard to see the connection to journalism there.

Joan C. Tronto, a trained political theorist and University of Minnesota professor who has written extensively about care ethics, takes an even broader view. In 1990, she and longtime feminist educator Berenice Fisher defined care as "a species activity that includes everything we do to maintain, continue, and repair our world so that we may live in it as well as possible."[5]

To analyze care practices more fully, they devised four phases of care:

1. "Caring about" is defined as identifying caring needs.
2. "Caring for" is about taking responsibility for meeting them.
3. "Caregiving" is the work of providing care.
4. "Care receiving" is how we know if the care was successful.

Care is about meeting needs, it is always relational, and it is not complete until the need is met, Tronto explains in her 2015 book, *Who Cares? How to Reshape a Democratic Politics*. Care requires constant reexamination of the situation and the resources assigned to improve it. That scrutiny inevitably leads to recognizing new needs, and the process repeats—endlessly.

"So care is a complex process, and it also shapes what we pay attention to, how we think about responsibility, what we do, how responsive we are to the world around us, and what we think of as important in life," says Tronto.[6]

Journalists spend their entire careers engaged in a never-ending care practice around information needs—identifying them, taking responsibility for them, meeting them, and gauging public response to our interventions. We just don't talk about it in those terms, if at all.

After I left the weekly *Roundup* for daily journalism, conversations about care—or, more specifically, minimizing harm—surfaced mostly when dealing with juveniles, survivors of sex crimes, or suspects not yet charged with crimes. Occasionally, we argued about whether our reporting was intrusive or voyeuristic; I recall one such time when I was assigned to get "neighborhood reaction" to the tragic deaths of five little girls who got trapped in the trunk of a car on a hot summer day.

We rarely, if ever, discussed how coverage would hurt or help a particular community, let alone communities made vulnerable by people, history, and systems that exclude and disadvantage them by design. It was only after I left newspapers for public media that I started to examine the relationships among local news, diversity, duty of care, and community well-being.

Listening

Journalism, as I have mostly experienced it, is rooted in scarcity. Reporters operate on the assumption that only a small subset of informed and connected people have crucial knowledge and insights worth amplifying. They listen mostly to people with status and power and their gatekeepers, and are rewarded for their ability to access and extract information from those sources. These are the people who effect change in the community. Everyone else is just someone affected by those changes, good for a reaction or opinion but rarely treated as someone with the power to solve a problem, let alone influence broader narratives. So, journalists spend virtually no time listening to them or trying to earn their trust.

> We rarely, if ever, discussed how coverage would hurt or help a particular community.

In 2003, American Public Media, parent company of Minnesota Public Radio (MPR) and Southern California Public Radio and producer of national programs and podcasts, created the Public Insight Network to fuel a journalism built on abundance, in which journalists listen to and engage with a diversity of sources and their reporting is informed by what they hear. In a profession in which journalists are constantly being told to do more with less, PIN was a way to do more with more, and my first job in public media was to expand it.

When I took the helm of PIN in 2008, the "future of media" discussion was dominated by talk of broken business models and promising tech innovations. What was often missing was a robust discussion about *listening*: how and why we listen, to whom we listen, what we listen for, and what we do with what we hear.

PIN set out to change that, to make listening to the community a priority in news gathering and to democratize expertise. It represented a social compact of sorts: if citizen sources would agree to share their knowledge and experiences, journalists would agree to listen and to use those insights to inform their reporting and to improve its context, depth, and accuracy.

It was both a mindset and a tool set. The mindset was a belief that everyone has knowledge to share and that diversifying sources and engaging communities can improve the quality and relevance of journalism. The tools included a database, survey builder, and an email provider that allowed journalists to target people based on demographics, geography, expertise, or interests and to capture their responses in a searchable, sortable database.

Over time, we trained 600+ journalists in 125 newsrooms to use PIN, and we grew the network to include more than 330,000 sources. As administrators of the system, my team had access to the responses from thousands of queries generated by all those newsrooms. Sifting through them every day was like reading a citizens' news wire that revealed not just what was happening in people's lives and in their communities but why they cared and what they were doing about it.

Specially trained public insight analysts in each newsroom would design questions to elicit insight, not opinion. They would ask, "What do you know about this and how do you know it?" not "What do you think about this and what should others do about it?" If they did ask for opinions, they asked what life experiences informed them. Analysts would then sift through the responses and present reporters and editors with story ideas, context, and sources. There was just one problem: reporters barely had time to pursue leads they had unearthed themselves, and some didn't appreciate analysts who heaped a document full of other stories onto the pile. Even journalists who were enthusiastic about using PIN did so mostly to find sources for stories already in the works.

When PIN was created, the founders wanted to reassure sources that the information would not be shared with fundraisers and marketers, so they promised sources that their insights would be seen only by journalists unless sources gave explicit permission otherwise. And so the vast majority of insights gathered through PIN remained locked in a database that journalists rarely accessed except as it pertained to the specific story they were working on or the question they were most interested in asking.

PIN was designed as a tool for journalists, not for communities, and that was its fatal flaw.

Reciprocity

There will never be enough reporters or enough time to pursue all news leads with or without an insight engine like PIN. In the end, scarcity is just more efficient. The fewer people you listen to, the easier it is to decide what to report on and whose power to center in your storytelling. And without an ethic of care to prioritize community-centered news, a system like PIN just ends up reinforcing the status quo.

By 2010, my team was thinking about how PIN could bypass reporters and benefit communities directly. We launched blogs.[7] We hired a commentary editor and a data visualization expert. We built a storytelling widget for libraries. And we facilitated conversations between and among people, allowing them to act on their own curiosity and share insights with each other. We thought, "Are there groups of people who should be talking to each other but aren't?" and then we helped create those exchanges.

In August 2016, for instance, we partnered with the Twin Cities chapter of the National Association of Black Accountants (NABA) to host "Women Empowering Women: A Conversation About Financial Security," an event at MPR's UBS Forum in downtown Saint Paul.

> Too much of what passes for engagement in news media puts journalists at the center of the conversation.

The idea for the event came from a PIN query that asked women how they are doing financially and what would help them do better. We heard from women working to overcome student loan debt, pay for childcare, save for retirement, live within their means, confront bias in the workplace, and have difficult conversations with loved ones about finances. We also heard from women with a lot of knowledge to share—about setting financial goals, creating budgets, negotiating a raise, and eliminating credit card debt.

When we asked the 170+ women what they wanted, the response, overwhelmingly, was to be in conversation with other women. Inspired, we reached out to our friends at NABA and asked whether they would cosponsor an event and help recruit their members to attend. About 25 women of diverse professional and personal backgrounds signed up and showed up, including a few MPR employees.

We did not record the event to broadcast, live-blog, stream, or to tweet it. It wasn't fuel for a news story. Instead, we ate dinner together and then spent an hour circulating among tables labeled with topics the women most wanted to discuss. We started each conversation by sharing stories about steps we had taken to better understand or improve our financial futures. We spoke about our relationship to money and the role money plays in our relationships. We talked about debt, divorce, and online tools for creating and maintaining a household budget. We talked about health care, retirement planning, and philanthropy, about obstacles we are facing and hardships we have overcome. And we talked about how to talk about all these things with children, parents, and spouses.

At the end of the night, we reflected on what we had learned and pledged to take one more action: write it down in a "memo to self" and seal it in a self-addressed envelope to be mailed back to participants in 30 days. Several women lingered to continue their conversations and swap contact information, and many asked why MPR doesn't do more of this.

One reason is that too much of what passes for engagement in news media puts journalists at the center of the conversation. People are encouraged to help reporters do their job, not help themselves or fellow citizens solve a shared problem. Increasing the number and diversity of sources willing to talk to media won't do much to strengthen communities or democracy if we don't coach journalists what to listen *for*—and by that I mean the work people are doing or willing to do to care for themselves, one another, their communities, and the planet.

This is what Tronto refers to as "caring with," or the fifth phase of care. The first four phases imagine a "citizen" as someone who is attentive, responsible, competent, and responsive, whereas "caring with" imagines "the entire polity of citizens engaged in a lifetime of commitment to and benefiting from the principles of caring."

"If democratic citizenship is to be truly inclusive, then we have to recognize that caring is what will get us there together," Tronto says.

If journalists' mission is to serve the needs of citizens in democracy, "you ought to be able to figure out what citizens do by looking at what journalists do," noted David Holwerk, the late scholar and director of communications for the Kettering Foundation. But when you look at newspapers, watch television, or listen to the radio, it's difficult to find citizens there doing anything, he added.

That's because journalists are used to listening for stories, quotes, or an opening in which to ask their next questions. We are less adept at listening for what citizens and communities need or the caring work they are doing and then rallying the resources to support them. When it comes down to it, most mainstream news organizations are in the story-producing business, not the community-caring business. They see community engagement as a means to an end—a way to share content and grow audience—when they could be using it to connect people to each other and their communities, and to create social capital.

Our collaboration around women's financial security showed that if newsrooms did a better job of listening for what people need, they just might discover it is something other than a news story. It might be a safe space for community members to inform and "care with" one another.

Subsidiarity

PIN, as a technology, eventually became obsolete. Twitter and Facebook proved less time-consuming as crowdsourcing tools go. By 2018, the code behind the PIN tool kit was fast approaching its end life, and with American Public Media prioritizing investments in podcasting and on-demand media, there wasn't much appetite or budget for upgrading it. Yet even before that, the principles behind PIN had propelled me to think differently about media's mission as a whole. I thought about what we could accomplish if we acted out of a duty of care—like a social enterprise, leveraging our capacity in storytelling, convening, and connecting to amplify critical social issues, build public will for change, and help communities to thrive. I considered the culture and systems that would need to change for that to happen and then got to work.

I rewrote my team's job descriptions to focus on engagement, equity, inclusion, and social impact more broadly. Together, we worked with the human resources department to formulate the business case for a more comprehensive diversity and inclusion strategy. We were instrumental in creating employee resource groups and ensuring that inclusion was added to the organization's list of core values. We expanded our portfolio to include impact evaluation. We sought collaborations with equity-minded organizations.

The most daunting of these collaborations was a yearlong project aimed at changing racial narratives in Minnesota media, the impact of which forever changed the way I view the industry and my role in it.

The project—dubbed Truth and Transformation: Changing Racial Narratives in Media—was launched in summer 2019 and governed by a coalition of six community and media partners. It was funded through the Saint Paul and Minnesota Foundation, and connected to the W. K. Kellogg Foundation's Truth, Racial Healing, and Transformation work. Our charge was to lead a narrative-change workshop and conference in spring 2019 that would assist Minnesota news professionals in uncovering their biases and amplifying community solutions to narrative change.

Whereas PIN addressed the question of "Who *informs* journalism?" Truth and Transformation also examined "Who *forms* it and who *benefits?*" It highlighted how a lack of diversity and cultural competence corrupt the mission of journalism, reinforce systems of oppression, protect privilege and Whiteness, and produce narratives that are inaccurate, incomplete, and inauthentic.

Most of all, it demonstrated that the people and communities most affected by problematic narratives know what needs to be done to correct them. In Catholic teaching, it's the principle of subsidiarity—the idea that the people who are closest to the problem need to be involved in solving it.

One of the most important aspects of the partnership was how intentional we were about centering the voices and power of individuals and communities routinely missing, marginalized, and maligned in mainstream, White-owned media—as well as amplifying the voices of journalists of color who often are asked to build bridges to these communities.

To inform the direction of the work, the partners convened 17 small-group listening sessions across the state in fall 2018. We wanted to know all the ways that communities of color and Indigenous communities experience inaccurate racial narratives in the media—and how to change it.

> The people and communities most affected by problematic narratives know what needs to be done to correct them.

We heard specifically how Minnesota media work hard to "comfort White people" by avoiding honest and nuanced reporting on matters of race and equity. We heard how college journalism programs are killing the spirits of students of color because they are being taught to tell stories in a way that is inauthentic so as to not offend White-majority audiences. As a result, they either drop out or get a job where, to survive, they must assimilate, into existing newsroom culture, perpetuating the same White supremacist ways of storytelling. And we heard a strong desire for journalists to operate through the framework of what makes a thriving community and to connect people with their neighbors and provide opportunities to explore individual and cultural identities, history, and contributions.

While many participants provided a number of recommendations for making mainstream media more responsive,[8] quite a few rejected the premise altogether. We don't need to help White-owned mainstream media to tell more accurate stories about us, many said.

We need our media, our own reporters from our own communities to tell our stories, people we can trust who are actually going to tell our stories with heart and with integrity.

We also asked, "What does it sound like, look like, and feel like to be accurately represented in the media? How would more accurate racial narratives influence how you experience public life and decision-making?"

They talked about how different public interactions would be. People wouldn't give them that "certain look," the one born from ignorance, fear, and disgust. They would greet them at a concert or convenience store. Younger participants in particular said it would also change how they see themselves and others, how it would illuminate their potential: maybe I can be a journalist; maybe I can work in media.

Finally, many participants said that more accurate and authentic narratives would help them feel connected and attached to their community. They would get more involved in civic life. More than one person said they couldn't imagine an instance where it wouldn't improve public life and their role in it.

Solidarity

One of the last big projects I worked on before leaving mainstream media was to help APM/MPR update its strategic plan, known as Audiences First, by coming up with a definition of relevance and a way to measure it.

We designed an ambitious listening process that included a survey of listeners who were also paying members; workshops with staff, community, and youth advisory boards; and focus groups with people who had little to no connection with the organization, mostly BIPOCTM (Black, Indigenous, other People of Color, and Traditionally Marginalized) young adults.

What emerged from those sessions were two distinct concepts of relevance. For staff and members, the majority of whom were White, relevance was rooted in *content and empathy*: something is relevant when it is useful, educational, satisfies my curiosity, expands my perspectives, and helps me see and connect to a broader world.

Our BIPOCTM advisors, youth, and focus group members talked about relevance in terms of *people, power, and solidarity*: we need you to have skin in the game, to know that our freedom is bound up together; we want space for connection and cocreation, where we can assist each other in a reciprocal way and build something together; we want to be producers, not just consumers; we want you to acknowledge our power.

It was clear that if the organization were serious about increasing its relevance, diversifying its audience, and broadening its contributor base, it would need to expand its mission beyond delivering quality content that "enriches the mind and nourishes the spirit."[9] It would need to do more than minimize harm. It would need to act in the best interests of the people and communities it was currently marginalizing and do it with them, not for them.

Just like the Truth and Transformation listening sessions, participants in our relevant focus group weren't all that interested in helping to reform White-owned media. They wanted—and deserve—media owned by people who look like them, who prioritize their needs and their communities' well-being in the same way so many White-owned and White-led media prioritize the information needs and comfort of their largely White audiences. In essence, they want solidarity journalism.

Anita Varma is assistant director of the Journalism and Media Ethics program at the Markkula Center for Applied Ethics at Santa Clara University, where she leads the Solidarity Journalism Initiative. Solidarity reporting, she explains, prioritizes the issues and information needs of communities that are disrespected or denied their humanity by centralizing the truth of people most affected by those issues. Here is Varma, writing about the history of solidarity journalism for the *Indypendent* in December 2021:[10]

> Solidarity journalism isn't new or niche—though it often isn't given its due in conversations about why journalism matters. In many countries, the origins of an independent press are rooted in viewing journalism as an act of resistance against state power that may otherwise deny that inhumane conditions endure within its domain.
>
> In the United States, we can trace the logic of solidarity reporting all the way back to mobilizing for independence, abolition newspapers that reported the truth and consequences of slavery for people living it (instead of focusing on those benefiting from it) and coverage of issues like child labor, factory conditions, suffrage, voting rights and immigration. This list goes on and continues today with a growing set of examples, like climate crisis reporting that focuses on communities affected and displaced rather than amplifying the preferred frames and excuses from companies responsible for it.
>
> We need more solidarity reporting because elite and official-focused reporting hasn't brought about accurate portrayals of marginalization. Vaccine inequity, labor

struggles, housing precarity and policing are making frequent headlines—yet all too often, the stories that accompany these headlines do not represent the people directly affected by these issues.

Toward a Caring Democracy

I am hardly the first to consider or write about the need for an ethic of care in journalism.[11] Nor are my thoughts about mutual care, listening, reciprocity, subsidiarity, and solidarity original or exclusive.

They are informed not only by my own experiences in journalism but by two decades of being in community with some of the most introspective, creative, and inspiring thinkers in the profession. One of those influencers is Cirien Saadeh, a community-trained journalist, educator, and organizer in Minneapolis.[12] She is the creator of Journalism of Color,[13] a resilient, transformative, and community-based journalism methodology that builds on the work of the Black and Brown press, narrative-building practices, theories of power and cooperation, as well as independent journalism, in order to confront and deconstruct hegemony.

In the aftermath of George Floyd's murder by Minneapolis police and the ensuing social justice uprisings around the world, Saadeh told me this about her efforts to embed journalism in social movements and about the duty of care that fuels her work:

> Have you ever watched *The Good Place*, the TV show? The questions they ask are: What is it that we owe to each other? How do we take care of each other? How do we do journalism that is built around mutual accountability?

I think about this in the context of food justice and food access in places like North Minneapolis and about the idea of mutual accountability. For instance, what is the role of food providers in building racial equity?

George Floyd was killed outside of a grocery store. During the riots, places like North Market and the corner store across the street were being protected by community members. Two of them are Arab-owned businesses, but then you've got a Black-owned business. You've got these other community-owned businesses that are all in this work together. And it led me to this question of how do we start talking about . . . this ethical, moral imperative around the care we show each other, and have those tough discussions in the news?

For journalism to be grounded in an ethic of care, we must acknowledge, as both Saadeh and Tronto do, that care is always infused with power and is therefore deeply political.

Every response to a caring need involves power relationships, and caring is political in that actors with unequal power come together to determine an outcome, Tronto says. Our duty, as democratic citizens, she argues below, is to guarantee that huge imbalances are rectified.

What makes care equal is not the perfection of an individual caring act, but that we can trust that over time, we will be able to reciprocate the care we received from fellow citizens, and that they will reciprocate the care we've given to them. In such an ongoing pattern of care, we can expect moral virtues to deepen: We will trust in one another in our social and political institutions, and feel solidarity with other citizens, seeing them as partners in our own caregiving and receiving.[14]

If information needs are care needs and journalism is the practice of meeting those needs, then a caring democracy demands that we correct the power imbalance around who informs, who forms, and who benefits from journalism.

By virtually every measure, Americans' trust in most of their democratic institutions, and particularly in the media, has declined dramatically over the past half century. Yet, for too many Americans, mainstream White-owned media have never had their trust to lose, and it's not difficult to figure out why.

In January 2019, as part of the Truth and Transformation project, MPR and its partners surveyed news media professionals in Minnesota about their perceptions and portrayals of various racial groups in Minnesota, the influence their work has on public perceptions of race, and their exposure to training about racial narratives.[15]

An overwhelming majority of respondents readily acknowledged their collective failure to accurately and fairly represent different cultural communities:

- 8 out of 10 media professionals said they have influence over public perceptions of Indigenous people and people of color while also giving Minnesota media a grade of "fair" or "poor" when it comes to representing these populations;

- 7 out of 10 said Minnesota news media rarely or never cite Indigenous people or people of color as subject matter experts for stories not explicitly about race;

- 9 out of 10 said racial biases among media professionals lead to inaccurate news stories;

- 9 out of 10 said it is important to learn about the race and culture of the people about whom they report and that understanding racial bias is helpful or essential to being effective in their job; and

- 8 out of 10 said it is "very important" or "extremely important" to receive training about racial bias and similar topics, and more than half said they did not receive that kind of training in school or in employer-sponsored trainings.

And despite all of this, the majority of Minnesota journalists surveyed said they were confident in their ability to report on racial and cultural groups other than their own.

What kind of reporting results from such cognitive dissonance? I'll give you an example from my own experience.

As a local government reporter for the *Salt Lake Tribune*, I once wrote a story about how Salt Lake County planned to spend $22 million in federal housing funds on revitalizing a single community known as West Millcreek. I remember the story very well because it featured an interview with a couple trying to sell their home and I used their story as an anecdote to explain why the county was targeting the area for investment.

The neighborhood, I wrote, "is marked by sagging single-family homes, whose owners can't or won't maintain them." I noted there were "no schools, no stores, no libraries, and, until recently, no parks." I quoted an economic development official calling it a dumping ground and a slum. And then I ticked off a list of statistics from the county's redevelopment study to prove his point, including the ratio of rentals (bad) to single-family homes (good), the poverty rate (high), the percentage of residents with college degrees (low) and "the dramatic increase in the number of divorced residents over the past two decades," the relevance of which escapes me, a divorced single parent. I portrayed people living in the community as helpless to effect change and government officials as the saviors.

Looking back, the entire narrative was inaccurate and harmful, told strictly through a deficit lens.

How different might the story have turned out if there had been an ethic of care to guide my choices? What if my editors and I had interrogated whose power was centered or decentered, whose voices were missing or marginalized, who benefited, and who was harmed? How different would the story have been if it hadn't been reported by a White cisgender woman working for a White-majority newspaper?

> How different might the story have turned out if there had been an ethic of care to guide my choices?

For democracy to work as it should, we need to reward mainstream journalists who initiate and participate in these conversations, but we also need to prioritize investments in media organizations that already approach their work as a caring practice.

To reiterate what participants in the Truth and Transformation listening sessions said: We don't need to help White-owned mainstream media to tell more accurate stories about us. We need our media, our own reporters from our own communities—people we can trust who are actually going to tell our stories with heart and with integrity.

BIPOC-owned and -serving media organizations have long played a critical role in the civic, social, and economic health of communities. They are connectors and convenors and trusted sources of relevant, actionable, and often life-saving information. Community-centered media are care-centered media, and they are as essential to a community's well-being as affordable housing, reliable transportation, and accessible capital. And yet the institutions we often turn to for funding critical community infrastructure—banks, community development finance institutions, socially responsible businesses, and government agencies—largely ignore community media as essential building blocks.

Correcting this is the focus of my work as director of the Equitable Media and Economies Initiative, a national effort to create a more just economy and caring democracy by investing in equitable community media. This initative is part of the Multicultural Media & Correspondents Association (MMCA), a Washington, DC-based nonprofit devoted to increasing media ownership among Black, Indigenous, and people of color.

When I launched the project in May 2020 at the University of Missouri's Donald W. Reynolds Journalism Institute (RJI), my aim was to spark new thinking and collaborative action aimed at "futureproofing" local media amid a public health pandemic, a news ecosystem plagued by underinvestment, and an economic imperative to address systemic racism.

In January 2022, RJI teamed up with MMCA to expand the project and integrate it with MMCA's broader strategies for increasing multicultural media ownership and changing harmful narratives through advocacy, coalition building, media business transformation, and celebrating multicultural media excellence.

The initiative's three main goals are to:

- equip local media to report on, contribute to, and compete in an inclusive economy;
- promote BIPOC community media organizations as critical civic infrastructure; and
- pursue partnerships, revenue strategies, and policy changes to fund them as such.

By examining harmful media narratives about the economy,[16] amplifying the work of journalists[17] and organizations[18] working to change that, conducting experiments with local newsrooms,[19] reaching out to the community and economic development sector,[20] and helping community media outlets tap into the billions of dollars that governments, corporations, banks, and community development financial institutions have pledged to invest in Black and Brown communities, we are leading a much-needed movement to fund BIPOC community media as a community development and caring strategy.

Simply put, more diverse media ownership gives communities power and resources to control their own narratives. It's a necessary means of correcting power imbalances and "caring with" communities.

"As citizens in a caring democracy, we would need to change not only the discourse about care, not only our own daily concerns with care, but political and social institutions to make them more caring as well ," Tronto says.[21]

This is what journalism needs. This is what democracy demands.

Journalism's Civic Media Moment Could Be a Movement

by Darryl Holliday

W hat do we see when we think about democracy? Literally, what do we see?

As a former beat reporter and photojournalist, I've often thought of the way imagery intersects with the words and emotions we ascribe to key events or influential ideas. I hadn't applied those insights to democracy, though, until media scholar Henry Jenkins raised that provocation at a 2007 conference to explore "What Is Civic Media?" After defining civic media as "any use of any medium which fosters civic engagement," Jenkins raised his personal concern about "what democracy looks like."

For most people, it looks like outdated images of colonial America—the American Revolution and the Boston Tea Party, or Frank Capra- and Norman Rockwell-styled images "consciously constructed by the popular front of the 1930s." Jenkins pointedly noted that our contemporary vision of democracy is rooted in the past. That's a problem.

"One of the challenging things about a center for the future of civic media is to imagine democracy itself having a future," said Jenkins, then codirector of the Center for the Future of Civic Media, which closed in 2020.[1] As a journalist, I believe that today's civic media are solving for a historic challenge: imagining journalistic processes that strengthen democracy rather than erode it.

Part of the solution lies in updating our collective image bank of democracy, and journalism plays a critical role in that process. Today, I don't doubt that images of Black Lives Matter uprisings and even the US Capitol insurrection would make it into an updated "image bank." In all likelihood, when you imagine democracy today, the imagery you see is from a news report on the latest mass action—from the pink, cat-eared, wool-knit caps of the 2017 Women's March and "I can't breathe" signs raised en masse for George Floyd to a single black Q on a white background.

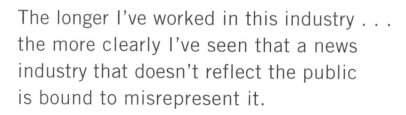

The longer I've worked in this industry . . . the more clearly I've seen that a news industry that doesn't reflect the public is bound to misrepresent it.

Societal change has always demanded collective, informed action—and news media, as in past periods of social upheaval, has undisputed power to shape the tone, tenor, and tempo of our public dialogue. On the ground, journalists serve as primary witnesses of civic action in that they are often judge and jury—deciding which imagery is shown, which voices are given a platform, and how complicated issues are perceived by a busy public. But editorial decision-making processes vary widely across news organizations, and the rules that govern journalistic production are often opaque to the public.

The civil rights lawyer Alec Karakatsanis quipped on this pathology in an excoriating social media post, in November 2021, in which he laid out the differences between "what mainstream media treats as urgent and the greatest threats to human safety, well-being, and survival."[2]

"Who is deciding to cover shoplifting with 'breaking news' urgency but not air pollution, wage theft, and fraud that leaves people and their children homeless and in poverty?" he asked. "Do the social and economic circles of journalists determine what they think is newsworthy?"

The simplest answer is, of course, yes. The longer I've worked in this industry—and the more I've grappled with the core questions of what and who makes journalism in the public interest—the more clearly I've seen that a news industry that doesn't reflect the public is bound to misrepresent it. How can local media understand and reflect a community when those who decide what's important to that community are so far removed from most of those who live there?

From the 1968 Kerner Commission Report[3] to the last American Society of News Editors survey in 2018,[4] study after study[5] affirms that the professional media workforce is, and has been, disproportionately White, male, able-bodied, and cis, and that it is made up of people who are significantly more wealthy, educated, and politically left than the people in their coverage areas.

Unfortunately, the top-down view from journalism's ivory tower shapes the view from the ground. To preserve their role as impartial observers, newsrooms, journalism schools, and journalism affinity groups have sworn a vow of "objectivity," a core tenet of journalistic professionalism that insists journalists not reveal their bias for or against either side of an argument. Paired with the media industry's unrepresentative demographics, journalism's obsession with objectivity often serves to normalize the perspectives of the same dominant groups that make up American newsrooms. Though designed to ensure fairness and nonpartisanship, objectivity often serves to protect the status quo when journalists themselves don't share the lived experiences of those most harmed by an objectively inequitable society.

As a Black man born and raised in the United States, I have never expected the commercial media industry to represent people who look like me. When a Black man or woman is featured in the news, it is likely to be in a crime story (as if police arrests represent the totality of crime), a feel-good story about people of color defying the odds (as if it's unusual), or a story of protest in varying degrees against institutional forces (as if all we do is struggle). I was assigned to write a version of all these stories during my time as a junior reporter. And while any number of these stories—from a range of decent writers—may be factual and well-intentioned, they are woefully incomplete, and they paint a picture of Black America that defines perceptions of individual people and communities across the country. This isn't solely a matter of journalistic priorities; it's a matter of how we understand and relate to each other—and who gets to add to our collective knowledge bank.

Who and what we see when we talk about democracy—and what types of civic information are produced in that democracy—are collective issues that we journalists can't solve on our own. That's why the best response to the current crisis in journalism is to get more people involved at a level on which everyone is willing and able to participate—not just as news consumers, but as distributors and, most important, as producers of local information.

I advocated for a more participatory public media in a 2019 Collaborative Journalism Summit keynote address, calling on the nonprofit media industry to move beyond the successes of engaged journalism" toward a journalism that informs, engages, and, most important, equips people with lived experience of the issues we cover to be news producers and distributors, in addition to consumers.[6] Later, I advocated for this in "Journalism Is a Public Good. Let the Public Make It," a 2021 *Columbia Journalism Review* special report that charts a path from the failure of commercial media to solutions focused on building public infrastructure through which everyone can find, fact-check, and produce civic information.[7]

Ivory tower journalism has failed. Journalism that works toward information equity must acknowledge journalism's top-down history, shift power to communities that have been left out of the public narrative, and embrace accountability for past harms. Then, it can truly be trusted to help define and communicate a shared vision for our democracy.

A New Deal

If effective democracy requires a free press, as the framers suggested in 1787, a new deal between the public and the press is overdue.[8] Local journalism that relies on community engagement, builds trust between journalists and the communities they serve, and centers on social, racial, and economic justice is needed in this time when trust in the institutions that impact the lives of millions of Americans is on the decline.

Journalists don't just define the visual image that we associate with a given event or time period; they write the narrative of our time. Journalists hold a great deal of power as stewards of accurate, actionable information necessary for the expression of collective desires and common understandings. As news media have become increasingly professionalized and commercial, cracks and chasms between the public and the press have emerged. While many Americans see skepticism of news media as healthy, according to a 2020 report from the Pew Research Center, more than half of all Americans think news organizations are opaque in terms of how they are funded (72 percent), where they have conflicts of interest (60 percent), how they choose and find sources (57 percent), whether a story is opinion or factual (55 percent) and, importantly, "how they produce their stories" (51 percent).[9]

It isn't just that the business model of journalism is broken; a new model built from the wreckage of the old may not be enough to save it.

In Chicago, the shape and color of a solution was illuminated in the Chicago News Landscape study, a survey of 900 Chicagoans and their perceptions of local media, published in 2017 by the Center for Media Engagement in partnership with my organization, City Bureau.[10] The study showed striking differences in the public's perception of media that correlated strongly with racial and geographic lines in the city where South and West Side neighborhoods are comprised largely of Black and Latino/Hispanic Chicagoans and where North Siders identify largely with the city's White population. South and West Siders were more likely to say that stories about their neighborhoods were too negative. They were more likely to say stories about their neighborhoods "quote the wrong people" and were less likely than their North Side counterparts to agree that stories about their neighborhoods "do a good job of showing what is going on." In addition, South and West Siders were less likely to have ever been contacted by a journalist than residents of Chicago's North Side and Downtown.

Yet, the same study found that, despite feeling poorly represented by—and disconnected from—Chicago news media, South and West Side residents were significantly more interested in taking action by volunteering with local news outlets in the production of local news and information (64 percent of South Siders and 67 percent of West Siders compared to 43 percent of North Siders).

While findings that many Chicagoans think they are underrepresented and misrepresented in the public narrative aren't new, the Chicago media landscape study affirms a public desire to help create more equitable, engaged local media coverage. Given the gaps that have emerged between the professional press and an increasingly diverse public, what shape might a new contract between the press and the public take?

It isn't just that the business model of journalism is broken; a new model built from the wreckage of the old may not be enough to save it. Today, the production of journalism is essentially controlled by an unrepresentative elite. Commercial journalism as a field of independent and consolidated media entities, established ethics, and public/private professionalization pipelines remains top-down and unrepresentative, rooted in profit and distanced from its stated purpose as public advocate and protector. The Fourth Estate can no longer claim its role as a critical component in a functioning democracy.

At the same time, new, participatory media organizations are countering decades of media corporatization, co-optation, and over-professionalization with networked, collaborative, and self-organizing models.

These new opportunities are not unpaid internships or opportunities for "exposure." At their best, they are acts of cocreation around common experiences. An excerpt from the executive summary of City Bureau's 2021-2024 strategic plan charts an evolution of news production at the Chicago-based civic journalism lab that we hope to see take shape across the country:

> As we learned and grew, our focus shifted from triaging gaps in the existing local media infrastructure to cultivating a new, more equitable and democratic system that could replace it entirely. Our experience shows that, to live up to its ideals, journalism needs many, many more people involved—not just as consumers, but as producers and distributors working in collaboration with professional newsrooms.

A growing list of nonprofit community-media organizations are bolstering local information ecosystems by working directly with communities most impacted by systemic injustice. From Canopy Atlanta, a community-led nonprofit journalism project:

> Our mission is to equip metro Atlantans to report in collaboration with experienced journalists about the issues their communities care about most. We tell stories that directly respond to neighborhood needs, partner with existing community information systems, and build neighborhoods' capacity to keep obtaining information from public records, officials, or archives.[11]

From Outlier Media, a Detroit-based service journalism organization:

> We identify, report, and deliver valuable information to empower residents to hold landlords, municipal government and elected officials accountable for long-standing problems.[12]

And from Resolve Philly, a highly collaborative organization dedicated to equitable news practices:

> Our work centers on improving how misrepresented communities are covered by the media. We believe that in a time of widespread mistrust, political division, and industry upheaval, journalists must reconsider not only what they report, but how they find, frame, and tell stories.[13]

It comes as no surprise that "civic," "community-led," "service," and "collaborative" are the words these organizations use to describe their journalism. The new public media eschew exclusivity, competition, and representative governance in favor of what the authors Jeremy Heimans and Henry Timms call "new power values" in their book *New Power*—open-source collaboration, opt-in decision-making, self-organizing, and networked governance.

To counter current threats to our democracy and address the problems facing our country, many of these organizations believe that journalism needs to adapt, borrowing from tried-and-tested approaches to public education, community organizing, movement-building, and civic engagement that cultivate collective change. The current local news media are struggling for finances, relevancy, and purpose, but, with innovation and investment, the collapse of the current business model could give way to stronger, more participatory media that are integrated with the local ecosystems they serve.

Upending Top-Down Journalism

At City Bureau our mission is "to equip people with skills and resources, engage in critical public conversations, and produce information that directly addresses people's needs. Drawing from our work in Chicago, we aim to equip every community with the tools it needs to eliminate information inequity to further liberation, justice, and self-determination."[14]

These empty meeting rooms are a point of failure for our civic information system and a critical missed opportunity for authentic democracy.

One of the places in which we've seen the clearest need for civic intervention is in the public's relationship to the thousands of public meetings that take place across the country every week. After all, Americans have the opportunity to vote for president every four years, but, according to our Documenters Network database—an online repository of dates, times, and official records from public meetings—there are about 600 public meetings held by government agencies and hosted by local elected officials every month, just in Chicago.

The 1976 federal Sunshine Act—officially at least—made public meetings workshops for democracy where local policy is shaped and where residents can witness, learn about, and act on the systems that impact their lives. Every day, in municipalities across the country, many of these government meetings happen with no oversight or input from the public. Although transparent by law, in practice, public meetings can be hard to find and difficult to follow without context. And as local newsroom capacity has diminished, the reporters who previously interpreted for the public are disappearing. These empty meeting rooms are a point of failure for our civic information system and a critical missed opportunity for authentic democracy.

Disengagement from public meetings is both a reflection and a cause of Americans' collapsing trust in institutions. Government that is hard to access is hard to believe, which creates fertile ground for misinformation.

It should come as no surprise that school boards have recently become the battlegrounds of choice for protesters who are "opposed to mask policies. Vaccine mandates. LGBTQ rights. Sex education. Removing police from schools. Teaching about race and American history, or sometimes, anything called 'diversity, equity and inclusion' or even 'social-emotional learning,'" according to National Public Radio education reporter, Anya Kamenetz.[15]

Public meetings also offer a unique opportunity for democratic renewal. Listeners can both reflect what they learned and change how officials behave, becoming trusted sources of information in their community. All that's missing is the right network of support to ensure that the transformational potential of public meetings is aimed at liberation, justice, and self-determination for all. With this new civic infrastructure, public meetings could become spaces for community alignment and honest disagreement about what liberation and justice mean at the local level, where people can engage and constructively challenge one another about their shared ideas and principles.

City Bureau is a civic journalism lab cultivating the information and storytelling networks that democratize access to civic power. Our vision for the future of local news upends the top-down model of journalism. It's a commitment that reframes the traditional consumer-producer relationship into one of cocreation, with journalists and communities working together to produce essential public goods.

Our Documenters Network trains and pays local residents to attend and document government meetings. It turns the knowledge, relationships, and capacity of local residents into a powerful community information resource through civic reporting, local newsletters, and online and in-person events. As of August 2022, this network is made up of more than 1,900 people who have collectively covered more than 3,000 public meetings.

Although Documenters vary in age (ranging from 18 to 83), gender identification (66 percent female and 8 percent nonbinary) and race/ethnicity (50 percent are people of color), the common link among all Documenters is that they want to help inform their communities.

Documenters across the country have reported a high degree of interest in developing new skills, getting more involved in their communities, and becoming producers and distributors of accurate information in their areas.

"When I go to municipal meetings in Chicago, I end up learning stuff that not only is information that educates me, but it also gives me and the groups I work with a chance to do more," says Cordell Longstreath, a 32-year-old educator, activist, and Documenter who moved around the Midwest before coming home to settle in Chicago's South Side Englewood neighborhood. And, he adds:

> I'm able to bring the information directly back to Englewood because if you just tell people the information, they'll start going to the meeting. So what I've learned is I have to go to the meeting and not only document it but actually learn what might be useful for my community and then go to specific people or groups and inform them. So that's how [I've] been connecting [my work and people].

Social scientist and public interest technologist Erhardt Graeff might call this "monitorial citizenship," a term originally coined by Columbia University journalism professor Michael Schudson, which Graeff describes as

> a form of civic engagement in which people collect information about their surroundings or track issues of local or personal interest in order to improve their communities and pursue justice. Common activities of the monitorial citizen include collecting information, sharing stories and insights, coordinating with networks of other civic actors, and pursuing accountability for institutions and elite individuals and their perceived responsibilities.[16]

Author and media professor Ethan Zuckerman agrees that "monitorial citizenship is a powerful way of holding institutions responsible that benefits from technology because it allows many people working together to monitor situations that would be hard for any one individual to see."[17]

While people may come into the Documenters Network with a monitorial citizen mindset, they leave (and return) with something more: the development of civic knowledge, journalistic skills, opportunities to practice those skills in a civic capacity, and the formation of interpersonal relationships that happens within a community of practice.

"The thing that I love the most—that I appreciate the most about City Bureau and that I think is special—is that journalism is a field that should be accessible to everyone," says Isabel Dieppa, a 37-year-old Documenter-turned-engagement reporter for the *Fresno Bee,* who knew she wanted to be a journalist but lacked the resources to afford the four-year journalism school she was accepted to after high school. She explains:

> Especially if you're low-income or rural and you don't have a local paper, you should be able to get the tools that you need in order to report on what's happening because people are passionate about their community. . . . I feel like what makes Documenters special . . . [is that] it's an open civics training that you can do a lot with. I learned a lot of skills that helped me to not just be a better citizen but also inform the type of work that I want to do.

Paid assignments emerge from this community but other, often unforeseen, assets emerge as well, the value of which can't easily be measured. These can include personal connections made via our Documenters-only message board, book clubs organized by and for Documenters, and Documenter-led webchats that provide a space where Documenters can share their skills and lived experience with other Documenters.

Daniel Wolk, a 76-year-old collegiate educator with a background in social and cultural anthropology, who has worked in refugee resettlements teaching English as a second language, had this to say about becoming a Documenter:

> I actually had very little experience going to public meetings. . . . I think that one reason why members of the public are in such a bad position to do anything about government is that we don't understand how government works well enough. We don't understand who's making the decisions and where they're making the decisions. And being a Documenter, you learn a lot about that.

Over time, we hope that tens of thousands of trained Documenters, who are trusted sources of civic information in their communities, will have transformative impacts on civic life in the form of more accountable local government, and that effective citizen oversight and legitimate public trust in institutions will lead to more engagement with elections and other civic processes.

Documenters and other community reporters should contribute to a systemic shift in how local media is produced, specifically by enabling people of color and others marginalized in existing systems to play central roles in shaping civic information.

A Promising Start

Drafting a new contract between the press and the public will take time.

A renewed movement for participatory, public media may be in its infancy, but it stands on the shoulders of public media movements that came before. A patchwork constellation of community information hubs already exists, woven into the fabric of their respective communities. Historically, these nontraditional community information conductors have been subsidized in varying degrees by public taxes:

- There are more than 10,000 public libraries across the country serving as living archives and real-time verifiers of community information. They are often the first and last resort for low-income and vulnerable people most in need of direct access to accurate, timely, relevant information, and they provide professional support for people on how to access it.

- The Alliance for Community Media has counted 1,677 PEG (public, educational, and government) access channels across the country.[18] These local TV and radio stations host trainings, produce local news, provide community meeting space, and build local connections.

- Similarly, there are more than 1,500 low-power FM stations owned by Indigenous tribes, religious groups, immigrant communities, and nonprofits across the country. Though they aren't always publicly funded, these stations are often highly participatory.[19]

- Finally, even though they don't fit the usual definition of mass media, there are more than 34,000 post offices across the United States.[20] As author and professor Victor Pickard points out, "These spaces could become centers for different kinds of community media, from weekly newspapers to municipal broadband networks."[21]

- High school and college newspapers, churches, block clubs, community organizations, and other civic and community-based organizations round out a networked community information service in the making.

A newsroom that connects existing civic assets around the participatory production and distribution of accurate, trustworthy, locally relevant information will build a future for local media as a true public good. No number of news articles will save us from the challenges ahead, but there are a million people willing to take on the role of "Observer" for the League of Women Voters,[22] "Court Watcher" with Court Watch NYC,[23] "Community Correspondent" with Model D,[24] "Info Hub Captain" with Resolve Philly,[25] or "Documenter" with City Bureau[26]—or any number of participatory media roles with public access TV and radio stations across the country. These people want to take action for their neighborhoods, blocks, buildings, or local newsrooms; they want to inform, engage, and equip their communities. So, let's build new newsrooms as civic hubs and integrate existing newsrooms into community spaces. Let's train many more people to commit acts of journalism without going into debt for a costly degree. Let's open up the field of journalism to include residents working alongside reporters on some of the biggest challenges facing our communities.

Imagine what kinds of data-gathering and community-based news products a network of thousands of people who care about their city could create if they were networked by a central, open-source technology and participated in journalism as a public good. Just as "citizen scientists" collaborate across the country to collect data and answer real-world questions on everything from lead pipes and light pollution to bird populations, a network of community journalists could monitor civic actions and institutions in a way that supports collective action. And what could we call this national community of practice? If that "network of networks" amplifies local voices and equips people with the skills needed to make and sustain change in their communities, we might call it a civic media movement or social movement, as Peter Block does in his 2008 book, *Community: The Structure of Belonging*:

> Collective change occurs when individuals and small, diverse groups engage one another in the presence of many others doing the same. It comes from the knowledge that what is occurring in one space is similarly happening in other spaces. Especially ones where I do not know what they are doing. This is the value of a network or even a network of networks. Which is today's version of a social movement.[27]

For years, commercial news media have failed communities across the United States, catering their resources toward content that serves the interests of the few and leaving many communities without access to the basic information needed to hold decision-makers to account between election cycles. This moral failing is built into the journalistic orthodoxy that consolidates power among already powerful private media entities.

In the coming months and years, as each US community navigates four interrelated crises—an ongoing pandemic, economic setbacks, systemic racism, and ecological disaster—journalism must generate new, noncommercial tactics to survive. Solutions that are not cocreated with communities most affected by these crises are at high risk of replicating the same inequitable infrastructure that has led the journalism industry to this point of sharp decline. Journalism that sees itself as part of a connected ecosystem can lead to a civic media infrastructure that is of its community. Paired with organized action, including community organizing, mobilization efforts, mutual aid, social movement building, and other levers for collective change, civic media freed from what New York University journalism professor Jay Rosen calls journalism's "view from nowhere" can better engage and connect vital and often disparate functions of democracy that inform traditional civic processes, from voting and petitioning elected officials to authentic mechanisms for collective problem-solving.

> Journalism that sees itself as part of a connected ecosystem can lead to a civic media infrastructure that is of its community.

As I noted at the start of this essay, Henry Jenkins suggested back in 2007 that one challenge to the future of civic media "is to imagine democracy itself having a future." I'd add that one of the challenges of democracy is to imagine a world where journalism has a future. Innovative news leaders and noncommercial newsrooms are springing up alongside community information hubs that have fought for years to preserve public media infrastructure. These information ecosystems are a bellwether for change that could point the way to a new civic movement in the United States—one in which people across the country play a critical role.

Contributors

Jennifer Brandel is cofounder and CEO of Hearken, a company that helps organizations around the world develop and operationalize participatory processes. She began her career in journalism reporting for outlets including NPR, CBC, WBEZ, the *New York Times* and *Vice*. Brandel received the Media Changemaker Prize from the Center for Collaborative Journalism and was named one of 30 World-Changing Women in Conscious Business. A Columbia Journalism School Sulzberger fellow and an RSA (Royal Society of Arts) fellow, Brandel also cofounded Zebras Unite, a global network of entrepreneurs, funders, investors, and allies creating a more ethical, inclusive, and collaborative ecosystem for mission-based startups. She also cofounded Civic Exchange Chicago, which brings together civic startups in a collaborative learning community.

Writer, journalist, and network builder **Darryl Holliday** is cofounder of City Bureau in Chicago, where he serves as a co-executive director of national impact. In 2019, he led the development of Documenters.org, an award-winning web app that pushes the boundaries of the traditional means by which journalism is produced and challenges the notions of who should have the power to report what happens. His writing and reporting have been featured in outlets such as the *Columbia Journalism Review*, *Chicago Magazine*, and the *Guardian*. Winner of the Rising Star award from the Reporters Committee for Freedom of the Press, Holliday's work has also been recognized by a Studs Terkel Award, a Sidney Award, and an Alfred P. Weisman Award, among others.

Michelle Holmes' work as an editorial writer, news executive, and producer of new ideas aimed at creating a more inclusive public square spanned two decades in American newsrooms and included leadership of the Pulitzer Prize-winning Alabama Media Group. In 2020, she opened Heart's Ease Love and Freedom Center, a new hub for collaboration with artists, journalists, healers, and facilitators. Heart's Ease functions at its core as a "feel tank" in a world of think tanks, using heart-centered ways of knowing to explore what it means to be free, while centering the experience of individual healing from cultural and individual trauma as a vital part of societal change.

Linda Miller is a seasoned communicator, collaborator, and capacity builder working to advance equity and create social capital through journalism. She currently leads the Multicultural Media and Correspondents Association's Equitable Media and Economies Initiative, a national effort to create a more just economy and caring democracy by investing in equitable, community-centered media as civic infrastructure. Previously, Miller spent more than 15 years as a newspaper reporter and editor and a decade leading diversity, engagement, and inclusion initiatives in public media. Miller has taught and lectured on journalism ethics and engagement at Arizona State University and the University of Utah as well as at the University of Wyoming, where she earned a BA in journalism.

Doug Oplinger retired from the *Akron Beacon Journal* in 2017 after 46 years working as a reporter and senior editor on education, business, public policy, computer-assisted reporting, investigations, and enterprise. During his time as editor, the *Beacon Journal* won two Pulitzer Prizes. He was also a member of the Knight Ridder collaborative team that won the Pulitzer for coverage of Hurricane Katrina. For five years, he led the statewide media collaborative, Your Voice Ohio, in experimenting with shared resources and community engagement for the purpose of representing people in local democratic practices. Oplinger is a graduate of the University of Akron and the Medill School of Journalism at Northwestern University.

A big fan of the value and joy of local journalism, **Eve Pearlman** worked in the San Francisco Bay Area for the bulk of her career as a reporter, editor, blogger, and columnist. In 2016, she cofounded Spaceship Media with a mission of reducing polarization, restoring trust in journalism, and building communities. Spaceship Media created a method known as *dialogue journalism*, which reconceptualizes the information and reporting process and puts divided communities at the heart of journalistic practice. Pearlman's work has since reached millions around the world through her popular TED Talk, "How to Lead a Conversation between People Who Disagree," and a book entitled *Guns, An American Conversation: How to Bridge Political Divides*, Simon & Schuster, 2020.

 **David Plazas** is the opinion and engagement director for USA TODAY Network Tennessee, which is part of Gannett Co., Inc., the largest news publication company in the United States. He has written award-winning editorials and columns on issues ranging from affordable housing to social justice to government accountability. He oversees the opinion team for multiple publications across the state, including the *Tennessean*, and hosts the *Tennessee Voices* video podcast. He also leads the *Tennessean*'s Civility Tennessee campaign on civic engagement and delivered a TEDx Talk in 2020 on the art and science of public disagreement.

 **Martin G. Reynolds** is co-executive director of the Robert C. Maynard Institute for Journalism Education. He oversees fundraising, external affairs, and serves as the institute's lead Fault Lines® diversity trainer. In 2010, he cofounded Oakland Voices, an award-winning storytelling project that trains residents to serve as community correspondents. His career with Bay Area News Group spanned 18 years and many roles, among them, managing editor and editor in chief of the *Oakland Tribune*. Reynolds was also a lead editor on the Chauncey Bailey Project, formed in 2007 to investigate the slaying of the *Oakland Post* editor. Reynolds is a professional lyricist and, among his many musical endeavors, was part of a live album recorded with his band, Mingus Amungus, in Havana, Cuba.

Ben Trefny is interim executive director of KALW Public Media, based in San Francisco. He earned a master's degree in journalism from the University of Oregon in 2000 and got his start in public radio at NPR member station KLCC in Eugene, Oregon. He joined KALW in 2004. Serving as executive news editor and then news director, he helped the station win numerous regional and national awards for long- and short-form journalism, much of it focused on community reporting. He also helped teach hundreds of audio producers, many of whom work with him at KALW today. Trefny is president of the Northern California chapter of the Society of Professional Journalists and also serves on the Journalism and Media Ethics Council at Santa Clara University's Markkula Center for Applied Ethics.

Subramaniam Vincent directs Journalism and Media Ethics at the Markkula Center for Applied Ethics at Santa Clara University. He writes and synthesizes research on the subject of advancing pro-democracy norms in the news media and is the author of several book chapters and journal articles. He was a John S. Knight Journalism fellow at Stanford University in 2015-2016. He cofounded and led two awarding-winning news magazines in Bangalore, India, and pioneered a hybrid citizen-professional reporting model. Vincent was originally a software engineer and lives in the Bay Area with his wife and daughter.

Editors

Paloma Dallas is senior program officer for international programs at the Kettering Foundation. She led the foundation's work at the intersection of journalism and democracy, working with journalists across the US and around the world to explore strategies for reinventing the teaching and practice of journalism to support thriving communities. For more than a decade, Dallas worked as an editor and writer, reporting on Kettering research and findings. Prior to working at the foundation, she was a freelance journalist; a reporter with Reuters in Bogotá, Colombia; and a researcher with the New York City-based Committee to Protect Journalists in the Americas program area. Dallas earned a BA in political science and Spanish at Macalester College and a master's degree in international affairs from Columbia University's School of International and Public Affairs, where she studied journalism with a regional focus on Latin America. She and her husband, an artist, have collaborated on many projects, including raising their daughter.

 Long known for her work in innovation and community engagement, **Paula Ellis** began her career as a journalist at several metro newspapers. She worked for 26 years at the Knight Ridder news organization as editor, publisher, and vice president of operations, after which she served as the Knight Foundation's vice president for strategic initiatives. She is currently a trustee of the Poynter Institute and a board member of the National Conference on Citizenship. For many years, Ellis has collaborated with the Kettering Foundation as a senior associate, working with innovative journalists from around the world on covering the news in ways that reduce polarization and strengthen both communities and democracy. In 2022, she expanded on those themes in a journalism textbook she coauthored, *News for US: Citizen-Centered Journalism*. Ellis earned a bachelor's degree in government and politics at the University of Maryland, and a master's degree from the Medill School of Journalism at Northwestern University. She is president of Paula Ellis Strategies, a consulting firm headquartered in Charleston, South Carolina.

Endnotes

Introduction

By Paloma Dallas and Paula Ellis

[1] Thomas Jefferson to Edward Carrington, January 16, 1787, in *Works of Thomas Jefferson in Twelve Volumes*, Vol. 5, ed. Paul Leicester Ford (New York: G. P. Putnam's Sons, 1904), 253.

[2] Quinnipiac University Poll, "Biden's Approval Rating Surges After Hitting Low Mark in July, Quinnipiac University National Poll Finds; Half of Americans Say Trump Should Be Prosecuted on Criminal Charges Over His Handling of Classified Documents," August 31, 2022, https://poll.qu.edu/images/polling/us/us08312022_ufcg18.pdf.

[3] Jeffrey M. Jones, "Confidence in US Institutions Down; Average at New Low," Gallup, July 5, 2022, https://news.gallup.com/poll/394283/confidence-institutions-down-average-new-low.aspx.

[4] Art Swift, "Americans' Trust in Mass Media Sinks to New Low," Gallup, September 14, 2016, https://news.gallup.com/poll/195542/americans-trust-mass-media-sinks-new-low.aspx.

Reorienting Journalism to Favor Democratic Agency

By Subramaniam Vincent

[1] Matthew Pressman, *On Press: The Liberal Values That Shaped The News* (Cambridge, MA: Harvard University Press, 2018), 6-15.

[2] Josiah Ober, "The Original Meaning of *Democracy*: Capacity to Do Things, not Majority Rule," *Constellations* 15, no. 1 (2008): 7.

[3] Sophia Rosenfeld, interview by Robert Talisse, "Democracy and Truth with Sophia Rosenfeld," March 16, 2021, in *Why We Argue* podcast, https://podcasts.apple.com/ee/podcast/democracy-and-truth-with-sophia-rosenfeld/id1205970945?i=1000513250528.

[4] Amartya Sen, *The Idea of Justice* (London: Penguin Group, 2009), xiii.

[5] Sen, *The Idea of Justice*, 324.

[6] Sen, *The Idea of Justice*, 337.

[7] Claudia Czingon, Aletta Diefenbach, and Victor Kempf, "Moral Universalism at a Time of Political Regression: A Conversation with Jürgen Habermas about the Present and His Life's Work," *Theory, Culture & Society*, vol. 37, issue 7-8, (2020): 19.

[8] Subramaniam Vincent et al., *Our Opinion: Recommendations for Publishing Opinion Journalism on Digital Platforms* (New York: News Quality Initiative, 2020).

[9] Daniel Hallin, *The Uncensored War* (New York: Oxford University Press, 1986), 116-118.

[10] Subramaniam Vincent and Don Heider, "Challenges and Opportunities for Local Journalism in Reinventing Political Coverage," *Journalism & Communication Monographs*, 24(4) (2022): 308-314

[11] Daniel Yankelovich, "The Bumpy Road from Mass Opinion to Public Judgment," *Higher Education Exchange* (Dayton, OH: Kettering Foundation Press, 2017): 21-28, https://www.kettering.org/sites/default/files/periodical-article/yankelovich_hex_2017.pdf. The article was drawn from Yankelovich's book *Coming to Public Judgment: Making Democracy Work in a Complex World* (Syracuse University Press, 1991).

[12] Sophia Rosenfeld interview, "Democracy and Truth," *Why We Argue* podcast.

[13] Tony Harcup and Deirdre O'Neill, "What Is News? News Values Revisited (Again)," *Journalism Studies* 18, issue 12 (2016): 1470-1488.

[14] Christopher Martin, *No Longer Newsworthy: How the News Media Abandoned the Working Class* (Ithaca, NY: ILR Press, 2019).

[15] Sophia Rosenfeld interview, "Democracy and Truth."

[16] Kim Phillips-Fein, "Countervailing Powers: On John Kenneth Galbraith," *Nation*, May 11, 2011, https://www.thenation.com/article/archive/countervailing-powers-john-kenneth-galbraith/.

[17] Christopher Martin, comment on "The News Media's Blind Spots Covering the Working Class," *Working-Class Perspectives* blog, posted September 23, 2019, https://workingclassstudies.wordpress.com/2019/09/23/the-news-medias-blind-spots-covering-the-working-class/.

[18] *Report of National Advisory Commission on Civil Disorders* (Rockville, MD: National Institute of Justice, 1967), 17.

[19] Pressman, *On Press*, 158.

[20] Christiana Mbakwe, "White-Supremacy Threat Demands Its Own Beat Reporters," *Columbia Journalism Review* (August 21, 2017), https://www.cjr.org/criticism/white-supremacy-beat.php.

[21] "White Nationalism/White Supremacy," *Mother Jones*, https://www.motherjones.com/topics/white-nationalism-white-supremacy/.

[22] Department of Homeland Security, *Homeland Threat Assessment*, (Washington, DC: Department of Homeland Security, 2020), https://www.dhs.gov/sites/default/files/publications/2020_10_06_homeland-threat-assessment.pdf.

[23] Kara Swisher, "An Asian American Poet on Refusing to Take Up 'Apologetic Space,'" April 1, 2021, in *Sway* podcast, *New York Times*, https://www.nytimes.com/2021/04/01/opinion/sway-kara-swisher-cathy-park-hong.html.

[24] David W. McIvor and Michael Rios, *Assets, Capacities, and Public Talk: How Communities Create and Negotiate Power* (Dayton, OH: Kettering Foundation Press, 2016).

[25] Derek W. M. Barker, "Deliberative Justice and Collective Identity: A Virtues-Centered Perspective," *Political Theory* 45, no. 1 (2017): 116-166, https://doi.org/10.1177/0090591715609407.

[26] Harcup and O'Neill, "What Is News? News Values Revisited (Again)," 1470-1488.

[27] Daniel Gilbert, "How Mental Systems Believe," *American Psychologist* 46, no. 2 (1991): 107-119.

[28] Daniel Kahneman, *Thinking, Fast and Slow* (New York: Farrar, Straus and Giroux, 2011), 20-30.

[29] Subramaniam Vincent, "How Social Media Has Harmed the Growth of Democratic Culture by Design," comment on *Berkley Forum*, Berkley Center for Religion, Peace & World Affairs, February 26, 2021, https://berkleycenter. georgetown.edu/responses/how-social-media-has-harmed-the-growth-of-democratic-culture-by-design.

[30] Yochai Benkler et al., "Mail-In Voter Fraud: Anatomy of a Disinformation Campaign" (Berkman Center Research Publication No. 2020-6, 2020), http://dx.doi.org/10.2139/ssrn.3703701.

[31] Hannah Arendt, "Lying in Politics: Reflections on the Pentagon Papers," *New York Review of Books* (November 18, 1971).

[32] Czingon, Diefenbach, and Kempf, "Moral Universalism at a Time of Political Regression," 33.

[33] The Solidarity Journalism Initiative, led by Anita Varma, has a sound theoretical and practical basis for how journalists can reframe their thinking about sourcing and storytelling.

[34] Kate Shaw and Leah Litman, "How Rights Went Wrong," interview of Jamal Greene, author of *How Rights Went Wrong: Why Our Obsession with Rights Is Tearing America Apart*, on *Strict Scrutiny* podcast, https://strictscrutinypodcast.com/podcast/how-rights/.

[35] Melissa Murray, "Open Wound," interview of Katherine Franke, author of *Repair: Redeeming the Promise of Abolition*, on *Strict Scrutiny* podcast, https://strictscrutinypodcast.com/podcast/open-wound/.

Journalism: Evolving with the People

By Doug Oplinger

No endnotes

Fostering Human Connection Is the Heart of Media Reform

By Michelle Holmes

[1] "12th Annual Shorty Awards," It's a Southern Thing, https://shortyawards.

com/12th/its-a-southern-thing.

[2] Actual names withheld for confidentiality. Comments posted on Facebook post, "Moms Can Solve Any Problem," 2019, https://www.youtube.com/watch?v=3Pw6jly4ZkE&t=17s.

[3] "Reckon South." Facebook page. https://www.facebook.com/reckonsouth.

[4] *Black Joy*, Reckon South, https://www.reckonsouth.com/newsletters/black-joy/.

[5] *Honey*, Reckon South, https://www.reckonsouth.com/newsletters/honey/.

[6] Sara Novak, "Humans Evolved to Be Lonely," *News* (University of Chicago Department of Psychiatry and Behavioral Neuroscience, March 28, 2022), https://psychiatry.uchicago.edu/news/humans-evolved-be-lonely.

[7] Richard Weissbourd, Milena Batanova, Virginia Lovison, and Eric Torres, *Loneliness in America: How the Pandemic Has Deepened an Epidemic of Loneliness and What We Can Do About It* (Cambridge, MA: Harvard Graduate School of Education Making Caring Common Project report, February 2021), https://mcc.gse.harvard.edu/reports/loneliness-in-america.

[8] Hannah Arendt, *The Origins of Totalitarianism* (New York: Meridian Books, 1951).

[9] UN General Assembly, Resolution 217 A (December 10, 1948), Universal Declaration of Human Rights, https://www.un.org/en/about-us/universal-declaration-of-human-rights.

Dismantling Systemic Racism in News

By Martin G. Reynolds

[1] Mark I. Pinsky, "Maligned in Black and White," Poynter Institute, https://www.poynter.org/maligned-in-black-white/.

[2] Elizabeth H. Hughes, "From the Publisher of the *Inquirer*: An Apology to Black Philadelphians and Journalists," *Philadelphia Inquirer*, (February 16, 2022), https://www.inquirer.com/opinion/commentary/inquirer-publisher-more-perfect-union-apology-20220216.html.

[3] Tema Okun, "White Supremacy," Dismantling Racism Works (dRworks), https://diversity.iu.edu/doc/anti-racist/resources-articles-lit/White-Supremacy-Culture-Tema-Okun2.pdf.

[4] University of Southern California Annenberg Center for Health Journalism, "Covering Unrest: When Journalists of Color Become the Target," June 10, 2020, https://centerforhealthjournalism.org/content/covering-unrest-when-journalists-color-become-target.

[5] "Mingus Amungus," Facebook page, https://www.facebook.com/Mingus-Amungus-80915214746/.

[6] "Charles Mingus," https://www.charlesmingus.com/.

[7] Michael Wines and Maria Cramer, "2020 Census Undercounted Hispanic,

Black, and Native American Residents," *New York Times*, March 10, 2022, https://www.nytimes.com/2022/03/10/us/census-undercounted-population. html?smid=url-share.

[8] "Stronghold," https://www.wearestronghold.org/.

Public-Powered Journalism

by Jennifer Brandel

No endnotes

Working *with* the Community

by Ben Trefny

[1] Mark Coddington and Seth Lewis, "Journalism Faces a Crisis in Trust. Journalists Fall into Two Very Different Camps for How to Fix It," Nieman Lab, October 8, 2020, https://www.niemanlab.org/2020/10/journalism-faces-a-crisis-in-trust-journalists-fall-into-two-very-different-camps-for-how-to-fix-it/.

[2] Kyle Pope and Emily Bell, "Introducing the Journalism Crisis Project," *Columbia Journalism Review*, June 17, 2020, https://www.cjr.org/tow_center/introducing-the-journalism-crisis-project.php.

[3] "Race and Ethnicity in the United States: 2010 Census and 2020 Census," United States Census Bureau, August 12, 2021, https://www.census.gov/library/visualizations/interactive/race-and-ethnicity-in-the-united-state-2010-and-2020-census.html.

[4] Denise Lu et al., "Faces of Power: 80% Are White, Even as U.S. Becomes More Diverse," *New York Times*, September 9, 2020, https://www.nytimes.com/interactive/2020/09/09/us/powerful-people-race-us.html?action=click&module=Top%20Stories&pgtype=Homepage.

[5] Thomas Edsall, "Journalism Should Own Its Liberalism," *Columbia Journalism Review*, October 8, 2009, https://archives.cjr.org/campaign_desk/journalism_should_own_its_libe.php.

[6] "Sights and Sounds of Bay View," 3rd on Third, https://www.3rdonthird.com/sights--sounds-of-bayview.

[7] "David Mathews," Kettering Foundation, https://www.kettering.org/people/david-mathews-president-and-ceo.

[8] David Mathews, *With the People: An Introduction to an Idea* (Dayton, OH: Kettering Foundation Press, 2020).

[9] "Fault Lines," Maynard Institute for Journalism Education, https://mije.org/

diversity-training/fault-lines/.

¹⁰ Oakland Voices, https://oaklandvoices.us/.

¹¹ Kat Ferreira, "Fruitvale after the Ghost Ship Fire," Oakland Voices, May 17, 2017, https://oaklandvoices.us/2017/05/17/kalw-sights-sounds-east-oakland-fruitvale-ghost-ship-fire/.

¹² Ben Trefny, *BOUNCE: The Warriors' Last Season in Oakland*, podcast, KALW, last modified January 14, 2020, https://www.kalw.org/podcast/bounce-the-warriors-last-season-in-oakland.

¹³ Renaissance Journalism, https://renjournalism.org/.

¹⁴ "Trusted Elections Network," American Press Institute, https://www.americanpressinstitute.org/trusted-elections-network/.

¹⁵ American Press Institute, https://www.americanpressinstitute.org/.

¹⁶ "Election Briefs," KALW, https://www.kalw.org/tags/election-briefs.

¹⁷ Ben Trefny and Sonia Narang, "The Bay Votes 2020—KALW's Live Election Night Coverage," November 9, 2020, https://www.kalw.org/politics/2020-11-09/the-bay-votes-2020-kalws-live-election-night-coverage.

Dialogue Journalism: Adapting to Today's Civic Landscape
by Eve Pearlman

¹ "About Eve," Internet Archive Wayback Machine, https://web.archive.org/web/20111205235316/http://alameda.patch.com/users/eve-pearlman.

A Framework for Building Trust with Communities
by David Plazas

¹ Cassandra Stephenson, "What Nashville's Rapid Growth Over the Last Decade Means for Its Council Redistricting Process," *Tennessean*, September 1, 2021, https://www.tennessean.com/story/news/local/davidson/2021/09/02/nashville-population-growth-demographics-census-2020-redistricting/5553923001/.

² World Population Review, "McMinnville, Tennessee Population 2021," https://worldpopulationreview.com/us-cities/mcminnville-tn-population.

³ Politico, "2016 Tennessee Presidential Election Results," December 13, 2016, https://www.politico.com/2016-election/results/map/president/tennessee.

⁴ Politico, "Tennessee Presidential Results," January 6, 2021, https://www.politico.com/2020-election/results/tennessee/.

⁵ Megan Brenan, "Americans' Confidence in Major US Institutions Dips," Gallup, July 14, 2021, https://news.gallup.com/poll/352316/americans-

confidence-major-institutions-dips.aspx?utm_source=newsletter&utm_medium=email&utm_campaign=newsletter_axiosam&stream=top&fbclid=IwAR2BML5qeNZwYtvZAI-DCMBkANHFQU75slaTlUqr-g1B9XKO4q6LyHPVfoo.

[6] Michael Anastasi, "We Know That Civility Is Important to Our Readers. That Is Why We are Continuing Civility Tennessee," opinion, *Tennessean*, November 24, 2018, https://www.tennessean.com/story/opinion/columnists/2018/11/25/civility-tennessee-michael-anastasi/2067461002/.

[7] David Plazas, "Donald Trump and the Will of the People," *Tennessean*, December 20, 2016, https://www.tennessean.com/story/opinion/columnists/david-plazas/2016/12/20/donald-trump-and-people/95645556/.

[8] David Plazas, "Reread 'Costs of Growth and Change in Nashville' Series," *Tennessean*, January 30, 2020, https://www.tennessean.com/story/opinion/columnists/david-plazas/2020/01/30/costs-growth-change-nashville/4605710002/.

[9] David Plazas, "We are Launching Civility Tennessee to Restore Faith in Each Other," *Tennessean*, January 14, 2020, https://www.tennessean.com/story/opinion/columnists/david-plazas/2018/01/14/we-launching-civility-tennessee-restore-faith-each-other/1023999001/.

[10] David Plazas, "Civility Tennessee Event Confirms Craving for Deep Connection," *Tennessean*, February 2, 2018, https://www.tennessean.com/story/opinion/columnists/david-plazas/2018/02/02/civility-tennessee-event-confirms-craving-deep-connection/1084401001/.

[11] David Plazas, "Why Can't We Hold a Civil Conversation on Race?" *Tennessean*, February 18, 2018, https://www.tennessean.com/story/opinion/columnists/david-plazas/2018/02/18/why-cant-we-hold-civil-conversation-race/335086002/.

[12] David Plazas, "How We Can Move the Gun Violence Conversation Forward," *Tennessean*, March 17, 2018, https://www.tennessean.com/story/opinion/columnists/david-plazas/2018/03/18/move-gun-violence-conversation-forward/425875002/.

[13] David Plazas, "Why Can't We Be More Civil on the Nashville Transit Debate?" *Tennessean*, April 14, 2018, https://www.tennessean.com/story/opinion/columnists/david-plazas/2018/04/15/nashville-transit-debate-why-cant-we-more-civil/509882002/.

[14] David Plazas, "Congratulations, Bill Lee. Here Are 6 Things You Can Do to Lead Tennessee to a Better Future," editorial, *Tennessean*, November 11, 2018, https://www.tennessean.com/story/opinion/2018/11/11/bill-lee-wins-heres-how-he-can-lead-tennessee-better-future/1910821002/.

[15] Elizabeth Grieco, "It's More Common for White, Older, More-Educated Americans to Have Spoken with Local Journalists," Pew Research Center, May 10, 2019, https://www.pewresearch.org/fact-tank/2019/05/10/its-more-common-for-white-older-more-educated-americans-to-have-spoken-with-local-journalists/.

[16] Media Insight Project, "A New Way of Looking at Trust in Media: Do Americans Share Journalism's Core Values?" American Press Institute, April 14, 2021, https://www.americanpressinstitute.org/publications/reports/survey-research/trust-journalism-values/.

[17] Trusting News, "Helping Journalists Earn News Consumers' Trust," https://trustingnews.org/.

[18] Braver Angels, https://braverangels.org/.

[19] Natalie Allison, "Tennessee Is Ranked 49th in Voter Turnout. Why Aren't Residents Voting Like They Should?" *Tennessean*, August 27, 2018, https://www.tennessean.com/story/news/politics/2018/08/27/tennessee-voter-registration-turnout-panel/1115860002/.

[20] David Plazas, "Join Discussion about Jon Meacham's Latest Book *The Soul of America*," *Tennessean*, June 11, 2018, https://www.tennessean.com/story/opinion/columnists/david-plazas/2018/06/11/jon-meacham-book-soul-america/690754002/.

[21] David Plazas, "On Civility: Don't Be Nice, Be a Good Citizen," *Tennessean*, June 26, 2018, https://www.tennessean.com/story/opinion/columnists/david-plazas/2018/06/26/civility-means-practicing-citizenship/735882002/.

[22] Adam Tamburin, "Manager Fired, Training Planned, Money Donated to Muslim Council after Ad Runs in *Tennessean*," *Tennessean*, June 22, 2020, https://www.tennessean.com/story/news/2020/06/22/tennessean-fires-manager-donates-funds-plans-training-after-anti-muslim-ad-runs/3234806001/.

[23] Samar Ali, "We Must Fight Hate and Disinformation Together: A Response to the Ad in *The Tennessean*," opinion, *Tennessean*, June 22, 2021, https://www.tennessean.com/story/opinion/2020/06/22/fight-hate-disinformation-response-to-tennessean-ad/3235351001/.

[24] Cameron Smith, "Welcome New Columnist Cameron Smith: 'I'm Conservative, Not Crazy'," *Tennessean*, June 23, 2021, https://www.tennessean.com/story/opinion/2021/06/23/welcome-new-usa-today-network-columnist-cameron-smith/7747942002/.

[25] David Plazas (@davidplazas), "I am on a call about leveraging our social networking strategy," Twitter, September 26, 2008, https://twitter.com/davidplazas/status/935771476?s=20.

[26] David Plazas, "How to Have (and Sustain) 'Adult' Conversations," TEDxNashville, YouTube video, December 17, 2020, https://www.youtube.com/watch?v=Oa9s1fMa8uw.

[27] David Plazas, "*Tennessee Voices* Podcast Tackles Issues of the Day in Coronavirus Era and Beyond," *Tennessean*, April 10, 2020, https://www.tennessean.com/story/opinion/columnists/david-plazas/2020/04/10/tennessee-voices-videocast-david-plazas/2955130001/.

[28] "Sign Up for Our Newsletter," *Black Tennessee Voices*, https://profile.tennessean.com/newsletters/black-tennessee-voices/.

[29] *Black Tennessee Voices* Facebook group, https://www.facebook.com/

groups/BlackTennesseeVoices.

[30] Alisa Cromer, "Connecting with Greater Nashville's Communities of Color," *Editor & Publisher*, November 19, 2021, https://www.editorandpublisher.com/stories/connecting-with-greater-nashvilles-communities-of-color,208133.

[31] Multiple authors, "Tennessee Black Writers Talk about Racism, Social Unrest and Next Steps," *Tennessean*, June 5, 2020, https://www.tennessean.com/story/opinion/columnists/david-plazas/2020/06/05/tennessee-voices-african-american-writers-racism-conversations/3137351001/.

[32] "Hallowed Sound," *Tennessean*, September 23, 2021, https://www.tennessean.com/in-depth/entertainment/music/2021/09/23/hallowed-sound-stories-perseverance-preservation-american-south-music/5617513001/.

[33] "Confederate Reckoning," *Tennessean*, https://www.tennessean.com/confederate-reckoning/.

[34] Adam Tamburin, "USA TODAY Network South Journalists Win National Journalism Award for *Confederate Reckoning*," *Tennessean*, June 2, 2021, https://www.tennessean.com/story/news/local/2021/06/03/usa-today-network-south-wins-national-award-confederate-reckoning/7528181002/.

[35] "Subscribe to the *Latino Tennessee Voices* newsletter," https://www.tennessean.com/story/opinion/columnists/david-plazas/2021/09/07/sign-up-new-latino-tennessee-voices-newsletter/5752395001/.

[36] Maria De Varenne, "We Will Reflect the Diversity of Our Community in *The Tennessean*'s Newsroom" editorial, *Tennessean*, September 1, 2021, https://www.tennessean.com/story/opinion/columnists/2021/09/01/the-tennessean-newsroom-will-reflect-the-diversity-of-our-community/5655138001/.

For Democracy to Work, Journalism Needs an Ethic of Care
by Linda Miller

[1] Pacinthe Mattar, "Objectivity Is a Privilege Afforded to White Journalists," *Walrus*, originally published August 21, 2022, updated February 10, 2022, https://thewalrus.ca/objectivity-is-a-privilege-afforded-to-white-journalists/.

[2] Rachel Abrams and Marc Tracy, "*Pittsburgh Post-Gazette* Staff Revolts Over Sidelining of 2 Black Colleagues," *New York Times*, June 10, 2020, https://www.nytimes.com/2020/06/10/business/pittsburgh-post-gazette-staff-revolt.html.

[3] "Code of Ethics," Society of Professional Journalists, https://www.spj.org/ethicscode.asp.

[4] Carol Gilligan, interview by ethicsofcare.org, July 16, 2011, https://ethicsofcare.org/carol-gilligan/.

[5] Berenice Fisher and Joan Tronto, "Toward a Feminist Theory of Care," in

Circles of Care: Work and Identity in Women's Lives, eds. Emily K. Abel and Margaret K. Nelson (Albany, NY: State University of New York Press, 1990), 40.

[6] Joan Tronto, *Who Cares? How to Reshape a Democratic Politics* (Ithaca, NY: Cornell University Press, 2015), 8.

[7] Paul Tosto, "Your Career. What Happened? Your Stories," *MinnEcon* blog, April 29, 2010, https://blogs.mprnews.org/minnecon/2010/04/your-career-what-happened-your-stories/.

[8] "Listening Sessions Insights," Truth and Transformation conference, 2019, https://www.truthandtransformationconference.org/listening-sessions.

[9] "About Us," American Public Media, https://www.americanpublicmedia.org/about/mission.

[10] Anita Varma, "What Solidarity Journalism Reveals to Us," *Indypendent*, December 22, 2021, https://indypendent.org/2021/12/what-solidarity-journalism-reveals-to-us.

[11] Linda Steiner and Chad Okrusch, "Care as a Virtue for Journalists," *Journal of Mass Media Ethics* 26, issue 2-3 (2011): 102-122. https://doi.org/10.1080/08900523.2006.9679728.

[12] Lolla Nur, "Meet Dr. Cirien Saadeh: The Unlikely Journalist," *Pollen*, https://www.pollenmidwest.org/stories/the-unlikely-journalist/.

[13] "About Journalism of Color," Journalism of Color, https://www.journalismofcolor.com/blank-page.

[14] Tronto, *Who Cares?*, 14.

[15] APM Research Lab, "Changing Racial Narratives in Media," July 1, 2019, https://www.apmresearchlab.org/racial-narratives.

[16] Mike Green and Linda Miller, "Journalists Must Play a Vital Role in Fixing America's False Economic Narrative," Donald W. Reynolds Journalism Institute, University of Missouri, October 6, 2020, https://rjionline.org/revenue-strategies/journalists-must-play-a-vital-role-in-fixing-americas-false-economic-narrative/.

[17] Reynolds Journalism Institute channel, "Reporting for a Post-COVID Recovery," April 21, 2021, https://youtu.be/QZPT87STVaE.

[18] Linda Miller, "Journalists, Business Leaders Consider Roles in Creating a More Equitable, Resilient Local Economy," Donald W. Reynolds Journalism Institute, August 17, 2020, https://rjionline.org/rji-partnerships/journalists-business-leaders-consider-roles-in-creating-a-more-equitable-resilient-local-economy/.

[19] Linda Miller, "Financing Multicultural Media: New Collaboration Positions Publishers of Color as Catalysts for Equitable Community Development," Donald W. Reynolds Journalism Institute, August 11, 2021, https://rjionline.org/news/financing-multicultural-media-new-collaboration-positions-publishers-of-color-as-catalysts-for-equitable-community-development/.

[20] Linda Miller, "Social Enterprise Leader Urges Local Media to Embrace the Role of Educator, Anchor Institution," Donald W. Reynolds Journalism Institute, July 29, 2020, https://rjionline.org/print/social-enterprise-leader-urges-local-media-to-embrace-the-role-of-educator-anchor-institution/.

[21] Tronto, *Who Cares?*, 28.

Journalism's Civic Media Moment Could Be a Movement

By Darryl Holliday

[1] "Goodbye," Center for Civic Media, https://civic.mit.edu/index.html.

[2] Alec Karakatsanis, "So, who is deciding to cover shoplifting with 'breaking news' urgency but not air pollution, wage theft, and fraud that leaves people and their children homeless and in poverty?" Twitter, November 26, 2021, 11:31 a.m., https://twitter.com/equalityAlec/status/1464270538998702091.

[3] Paul Delaney, "Kerner Report at 50: Media Diversity Still Decades Behind," *USA Today*, March 20, 2018, https://www.usatoday.com/story/money/nation-now/2018/03/20/kerner-report-50-media-diversity-still-decades-behind/1012047001/.

[4] American Society of News Editors, "How Diverse Are US Newsrooms?" 2018, https://googletrends.github.io/asne/.

[5] Derek Thompson, "Report: Journalists Are Miserable, Liberal, Over-Educated, Under-Paid, Middle-Aged Men (Mostly)," *Atlantic*, May 8, 2014, https://www.theatlantic.com/business/archive/2014/05/report-journalists-are-miserable-over-educated-under-paid-middle-aged-men-mostly/361891/.

[6] Darryl Holliday, "Don't Just Engage, Equip," City Bureau, May 18, 2019, https://medium.com/city-bureau/dont-just-engage-equip-7dfc9fe0d3b.

[7] Darryl Holliday, "Journalism Is a Public Good. Let the Public Make It," *Columbia Journalism Review*, December 15, 2021, https://www.cjr.org/special_report/journalism-power-public-good-community-infrastructure.php.

[8] Constitution Annotated, "Amendment 1.3.1: Historical Background of Free Speech Clause," https://constitution.congress.gov/browse/essay/amdt1-3-1/ALDE_00013537/#:~:text=3.1%20Freedom%20of%20Press%3A%20Overview,-First%20Amendment%3A&text=Congress%20shall%20make%20no%20law,for%20a%20redress%20of%20grievances.

[9] Jeffrey Gottfried, Mason Walker, and Amy Mitchell, "Americans See Skepticism of News Media as Healthy, Say Public Trust in the Institution Can Improve," Pew Research Center, August 31, 2020, https://www.pewresearch.org/journalism/2020/08/31/americans-see-skepticism-of-news-media-as-healthy-say-public-trust-in-the-institution-can-improve/.

[10] Jay Jennings, Natalie Jomini Stroud, and Emily Van Duyn, "Chicago News Landscape," University of Texas at Austin Center for Media Engagement, January 10, 2018, https://mediaengagement.org/research/chicago-news-landscape/.

[11] "About," Canopy Atlanta, https://canopyatlanta.org/about/.

[12] "About Outlier," Outlier Media, https://outliermedia.org/about-outlier/.

[13] Resolve Philly, https://resolvephilly.org/.

[14] "Our Mission and Vision," City Bureau, https://www.citybureau.org/our-

mission#:~:text=Our%20Mission%20%26%20Vision,that%20directly%20 addresses%20people's%20needs.

[15] Anya Kamenetz, "A Look at the Groups Supporting School Board Protesters Nationwide," National Public Radio, October 26, 2021, https://www. npr.org/2021/10/26/1049078199/a-look-at-the-groups-supporting-school-board-protesters-nationwide.

[16] Erhardt Graeff, "Monitorial Citizenship," in *The International Encyclopedia of Media Literacy*, eds. R. Hobbs and P. Mihailidis, John Wiley & Sons, Inc., 2019, 1-15.

[17] Ethan Zuckerman, "Insurrectionist Civics in the Age of Mistrust," blog, October 19, 2015, https://ethanzuckerman.com/2015/10/19/insurrectionist-civics-in-the-age-of-mistrust/.

[18] "Find Community Media," Alliance for Community Media, https://www. allcommunitymedia.org/ACM/News/Presidents_Messages/2020/05-May/www. allcommunitymedia.org/ACM/About/Community_Media_Directory/ACM/ Directory/Community_Media_Directory.aspx?hkey=8936f226-f206-43fd-b24e-2b4b337e1af0.

[19] Nancy Vogt, "Number of US Low-Power FM Radio Stations Has Nearly Doubled Since 2014," Pew Research Center, September 19, 2016, https://www. pewresearch.org/fact-tank/2016/09/19/number-of-u-s-low-power-fm-radio-stations-has-nearly-doubled-since-2014/.

[20] Martin Placek, "United States Postal Service's Total Number of Post Offices from FY 2015 to FY 2021," Statista, April 12, 2022, https://www. statista.com/statistics/943334/usps-number-of-post-offices/.

[21] Victor Pickard, "Instead of Killing the US Postal Service, Let's Expand It," *Nation*, May 7, 2020, https://www.thenation.com/article/society/usps-funding-local-media/.

[22] League of Women Voters, *Observing Your Government in Action: Protecting Your Right to Know* (Washington, DC: League of Women Voters, 2007), https://www.lwv.org/sites/default/files/2018-05/lwvef_ observingyourgovernment.pdf.

[23] "About Court Watch NYC," https://www.courtwatchnyc.org/.

[24] David Sands, "These 6 Detroiters Will Share Stories About Their Neighborhoods as Model D Community Correspondents," Model D, October 20, 2020, https://www.modeldmedia.com/features/community-correspondents-bios.aspx.

[25] Lily Medosch, Gabriela Rivera, Kristine Villanueva, "How Resolve Philly's Equally Informed Bridges the City's Digital Divide," Resolve Philly, May 7, 2021, https://medium.com/resolvephilly/how-resolve-phillys-equally-informed-bridges-the-city-s-digital-divide-4d199caf72b3.

[26] "Documenters," City Bureau, https://www.documenters.org/.

[27] Peter Block, *Community: The Structure of Belonging* (San Francisco: Berrett-Koehler Publishers, 2008), 75.